C000071928

Apache

P H R A S E B O O K

ESSENTIAL CODE AND COMMANDS

Daniel Lopez
Jesus Blanco

DEVELOPER'S LIBRARY

Sams Publishing, 800 East 96th Street, Indianapolis, Indiana 46240 USA

Acquisitions Editor Shelley Johnston	**Project Editor** Mandie Frank	**Proofreaders** Charlotte Clapp Leslie Joseph	**Multimedia Developer** Dan Scherf
Development Editor Damon Jordan	**Production Editor** Ben Berg	**Technical Editor** Aron Hsiao	**Book Designer** Gary Adair
Managing Editor Patrick Kanouse	**Indexers** Aaron Black Cheryl Lenser	**Publishing Coordinator** Vanessa Evans	

Table of Contents

Contents

About the Authors

Daniel Lopez is the founder and CTO of BitRock, a technology company providing multiplatform installation and management tools for a variety of commercial and open source software products.

Previously, he was part of the original engineering team at Covalent Technologies, Inc., which provides Apache software support and services for the enterprise. He is the author of several popular Apache and Linux guides, the mod_mono module for integrating Apache and .NET, and Comanche—a GUI configuration tool for Apache. Daniel is a regular speaker at open source conferences such as LinuxWorld, ApacheCon, and the O'Reilly Open Source Convention. He holds a master's of science degree in telecommunications from the Escuela Superior de Ingenieros de Sevilla and Danmarks Tekniske Universitet. Daniel is a member of the Apache Software Foundation.

Jesus Blanco is project manager for BitRock, a technology company that provides multiplatform installation and management tools for a variety of commercial and open source software products. Before joining BitRock, Jesus's position with the Spanish Institute of Foreign Commerce led him to projects in Brazil, France, Germany, Portugal, and much of Southeast Asia. Jesus is also a contributor to the Apache Documentation project and has translated much of the Apache documentation into Spanish. He holds a business administration degree from University of Seville and a master's in computer science from UNED.

Dedication

To Erica and Marisol, for your love and support.

Acknowledgments

First of all, I want to thank my editor, Shelley Johnston. She is living proof that human patience knows no limits, and through her enthusiasm and drive she kept the book on course, despite our busy work schedule and delays. I want to thank my co-author, Jesus, and business partner, Erica, for the time and effort they spent making this book happen. Writing a book while working full time on a software startup can be quite stressful at times, so a special thanks goes to my girlfriend and family, for their support.

Finally, I want to say "Hola" and thank you to my awesome team that makes BitRock such a great place to work.

We Want to Hear from You!

As the reader of this book, *you* are our most important critic and commentator. We value your opinion and want to know what we're doing right, what we could do better, what areas you'd like to see us publish in, and any other words of wisdom you're willing to pass our way.

You can email or write me directly to let me know what you did or didn't like about this book—as well as what we can do to make our books stronger.

Please note that I cannot help you with technical problems related to the topic of this book, and that due to the high volume of mail I receive, I might not be able to reply to every message.

When you write, please be sure to include this book's title and author as well as your name and phone or email address. I will carefully review your comments and share them with the author and editors who worked on the book.

E-mail: webdev@samspublishing.com

Mail: Mark Taber
Associate Publisher
Sams Publishing
800 East 96th Street
Indianapolis, IN 46240 USA

Reader Services

Visit our website and register this book at **www. samspublishing.com/register** for convenient access to any updates, downloads, or errata that might be available for this book.

Introduction

Apache has always been at the core of the Web, from its modest beginnings as a fork of the NCSA server to the latest version that's packed with features. Over time it has grown in both capability and complexity to the point that it can be overwhelmingly intimidating to newcomers. The goal of this book is to help you navigate Apache's hundreds of options, as well as serve as a gentle introduction and handy cheat-sheet for common tasks. Just as a language phrasebook can be a priceless companion when visiting a foreign country—helping you order food or ask for directions—I hope this *Apache Phrasebook* will be useful to you when configuring your web servers.

Apache Phrasebook provides guidance and snippets so you can customize Apache to suit your individual needs. There is more to Apache, of course, than can be covered in a book this size. When you register this book at www.samspublishing.com/register, you will find more content to complement it and highlight the most commonly used and not-so-common (but still useful) features of the server.

## 1

Apache Basics

Discovering Apache

This chapter provides a quick introduction to the
Apache web server, its architecture, and the differences
between major versions (1.3, 2.x). It explains how to
download and compile Apache from source or using
binary packages, how to enable or disable common
modules, the layout of server files, and the structure
and syntax of the server configuration files. It also covers how to start/stop/restart Apache and the minimum
configuration changes required to get Apache up and
running.

Apache is the most popular web server on the
Internet, with around 68% of the market share, according to Netcraft (http://www.netcraft.com).

Apache is

- **Portable**—It runs on Linux, Windows, Mac OS
  X, and many other operating systems.

- **Flexible**—It has a modular, extensible architecture and can be configured in a variety of ways.
- **Open Source**—You can download and use Apache for free. Availability of the source code means you can create custom builds of Apache.

There are two main versions of Apache in widespread use today: the 1.3 series and the 2.x series.

Apache 2.0 includes a number of improvements and features over Apache 1.3; however, it is incompatible with all modules written for Apache 1.3. As a basic rule of thumb, use Apache 2.x if you

- Are running a Windows operating system.
- Need to serve a lot of static content that can benefit from a threaded processing module on Unix.
- Need one of the new features only available in Apache 2.0.
- Are completely new to Apache.

Run Apache 1.3 if you

- Need to run in-house or third-party modules that have not yet been ported to Apache 2.x.
- Need to run software such as PHP with non-thread-safe extensions (though the same code will probably run equally well on Apache 2.0 with the prefork MPM).
- Are already familiar with Apache 1.3 and have no specific need to upgrade.

Determining Whether Apache Is Already Installed

```
rpm -q httpd
rpm -q apache
rpm -q apache2
```

If you are running a Linux system, chances are that Apache is already installed. If your distribution uses the rpm package management system, you can check to see whether Apache is installed with the preceding commands. There are several different commands because not all distributions use the same name for packages.

In most Unix-like systems, including Mac OS X, you can also directly check whether the Apache binary is installed with one of

```
httpd -v
/usr/sbin/httpd -v
```

If found, it should return something similar to

```
Server version: Apache/2.0.54
Server built:   Apr 16 2005 14:25:31
```

You can get an even more detailed response using `httpd -V`.

On Windows systems, you can check whether Apache is installed in the Add/Remove Programs section of the Control Panel. The installation path is under `C:\Program Files\Apache Group`.

Where Can I Get Apache?

Apache is included by default in most Linux distributions and in Mac OS X. You can also download binaries and source code for a variety of platforms, including Windows, from the official Apache website at http://www.apache.org.

Installing Apache 1.3 on Linux and Unix

```
tar xvfz apache_1.3.33.tar.gz
cd apache_1.3.33
./configure --prefix=/usr/local/apache --enable-
shared=max
make
make install
```

You can use the package management tools of your operating system to install pre-built versions of the server. This is often preferred because they integrate well with the existing file system layout and with other vendor-provided packages. It is, however, important to know how to build your own version of Apache from source code. This will allow you, for example, to build a server customized to your needs as well as to quickly apply security patches as they are released.

The first step is to visit the http://httpd.apache.org website and download the appropriate source tarball. When referring to 1.3-specific functionality, the rest of the book assumes you installed Apache 1.3.33. That is the most recent version in the 1.3 series at the time of this writing. The source tarball will be named apache_1.3.33.tar.gz.

You can now uncompress, configure, compile, and install Apache with the commands in the preceding listing.

The option --prefix indicates the path under which the server will be installed and --enable-shared=max activates loadable module support. Loadable module support is necessary to extend or customize the functionality later on without having to recompile the server.

NOTE: You may find Apache releases with a .tar.bz2 ending. This means that they were compressed with the bzip2 tool. While slower to compress and decompress, this format can reduce the size of the distribution files and is now commonly used by many open source projects. To decompress this kind of file, you can do one of the following on most modern Linux systems:

```
bunzip2 < apache_1.3.33.tar.bz2 | tar xvf -
tar xvfj apache_1.3.33.tar.bz2
```

Installing Apache 2.0 on Linux and Unix

```
tar xvfz apache_2.0.54.tar.gz
cd apache_2.0.54
./configure --prefix=/usr/local/apache --enable-so -
-enable-mods-shared=most
make
make install
```

The process is similar to the one described earlier for 1.3, though the options to enable support for loadable modules are different.

Installing Apache on Windows

Installing Apache on Windows is even easier than on Unix. The installation process for both Apache 1.3 and 2.x is quite similar. You simply need to download and launch the binary installer package from http://httpd.apache.org.

The wizard will ask you where to install the server and a few other pieces of information:

- The network domain name
- The fully qualified domain name of the server
- The administrator's email address

The server name will be the name that your clients will use to access your server. The email address will be displayed in error messages so that visitors know how to contact you if there is a problem. You will also be offered the choice of running Apache as a service. That option is appropriate if you require Apache to always run when the server boots up, for example. Otherwise, you can always start Apache from the command line.

Can I Install Different Versions of Apache on the Same Machine?

Yes, it is entirely possible, and there are many reasons why you may want to do so. You just need to pick up different installation prefixes. For example, you may want to install an Apache 1.3 server under /usr/local/apache and a 2.0 server under /usr/local/apache2. If you want to run the servers simultaneously, you will need to make sure they use different address and port combinations.

Remember that you don't need to install multiple Apache servers if you just want to run different websites. It is possible to do so with only one Apache server by using the virtual hosts feature, discussed in Chapter 5.

It is also possible to have several servers, each one of them serving a separate part of a website. For example, you can have an Apache 2.0 server providing the main www.example.com website content and delegate the content under www.example.com/signup/ to an Apache 1.3 server running a legacy mod_perl application. You can do so using a reverse proxy, as explained in Chapter 10.

Configuration File Basics

The following table provides the default location of the main Apache configuration file on multiple operating systems. Notice that since versions 1.3 and 2 of the server may need to coexist side by side, the name of the file may be different for each version.

Table 1.1   The Location of httpd.conf on Different Systems

Configuration File Location	Platform
/etc/httpd/httpd.conf /etc/httpd/httpd2.conf	Suse, Mandrake, older Red Hat systems
/etc/httpd/conf/httpd.conf /etc/httpd/conf/httpd2.conf	Newer Red systems, Fedora Core
/usr/local/apache2/conf /usr/local/apache/conf	When compiling from source as explained earlier in this chapter
c:\Program Files\Apache Group\Apache2\conf\httpd.conf c:\Program Files\Apache Group\Apache2\conf\httpd.conf	Windows
/private/etc/httpd/httpd.conf	Mac OS X

The main Apache configuration file is called
httpd.conf. The location of this file varies depending
on whether you are using Windows or Linux, and
whether you compiled Apache from source code or
used the binary provided by your distribution. Check
the locations suggested in the previous table.

Apache uses plain text files for configuration. The configuration files can contain directives and containers
(also known as "sections"). You can place comments
inside the file by placing a hash mark (#) at the beginning of a line. Comment lines will be ignored by
Apache. A directive can span several lines if you end
the previous line with a backslash character (\).

Directives control every aspect of the server. You can
place directives inside containers, so they only apply to
content served from a certain directory or location,
requests served by a particular virtual host, and so on.

When an argument to a directive is a relative path, it is
assumed to be relative to the server installation path
(server root). For example, if you installed Apache from
source as described earlier in this chapter, the server
root is /usr/local/apache or /usr/local/apache2. You
can change the default with the ServerRoot directive.

Using Multiple Configuration Files

```
Include /etc/httpd/conf/perl.conf
Include conf.d/*.conf
Include siteconf/
```

It is sometimes useful to split the server configuration
into multiple files. The Include directive allows you to

include individual files, all of the files in a particular directory, or files matching a certain pattern, as shown in these examples. If a relative path is specified, then it will be considered relative to the path specified by the ServerRoot directive.

This is usually done by Linux distributions that distribute Apache modules as RPMs. Each one of those packages can place its own configuration file in a specific directory, and Apache will automatically pick it up.

Starting, Stopping, and Restarting Apache

```
apachectl start
apachectl stop
apachectl restart
apachectl graceful
```

To start, stop, or restart Apache, you can issue any of these commands. Depending on how you installed Apache, you may need to provide an absolute path to apachectl, such as /usr/sbin/apachectl or /usr/local/apache/bin/apachectl. Although it is possible to control Apache on Unix using the httpd binary directly, it is recommended that you use the apachectl tool. The apachectl support program is distributed as part of Apache and wraps common functionality in an easy-to-use script.

On Unix, if Apache binds to a privileged port (those between 1–1024), you will need root privileges to start the server.

If you make some changes to the configuration files and you want them to take effect, it is necessary to signal Apache that the configuration has changed. You can do this by stopping and starting the server, by sending a restart signal, or by performing a graceful restart. This tells Apache to reread its configuration. To learn the difference between a regular restart and a graceful restart, please read the next section.

As an alternative to using the apachectl script, you can use the kill command directly to send signals to the parent Apache process. This is explained in detail in the "Alternate Ways of Stopping Apache" section in Chapter 2.

On Windows, you can signal Apache directly using the apache.exe executable:

```
apache.exe -k restart
apache.exe -k graceful
apache.exe -k stop
```

You can access shortcuts to these commands in the Start menu entries that the Apache installer created. If you installed Apache as a service, you can start or stop Apache by using the service management tools in Windows as follows: In Control Panel, select Administrative Tasks, and then click on the Services icon.

Additionally, Apache 2.0 can place a program, Apache Monitor, in the system tray. It is a simple GUI that you can use to start and stop the server directly or as a service. It is either installed at startup or you can launch it from the Apache entry in the Start menu.

What Is a Graceful Restart?

A "regular" restart stops the Apache server and starts it again. As a result, current requests are aborted and no new requests are served until the server is up and running again. Therefore, a normal restart can result in a momentary pause of service.

A graceful restart takes a different approach. Each thread or process serving a client will keep processing the current request, but when it is finished, it will be killed and replaced by a new thread or process with the new configuration. This allows seamless operation of the web server with no downtime.

The most practical way of performing a graceful restart in Unix is issuing the following command:

```
# apachectl graceful
```

In Windows, use

```
Apache.exe -k graceful
```

Changing the Address and Port Apache Uses

```
Listen 192.168.200.4:80
Listen 8080
```

Apache needs to know in which IP addresses and ports to listen for incoming requests. You can specify those using the Listen directive. The Listen directive takes a port to listen to and (optionally) an IP address. If no IP address is specified, Apache will use all available IP addresses. In this example, Apache will listen for requests on port 80 at the IP address 192.168.200.4 and on port 8080 at all available addresses. You can use

multiple Listen directives to specify multiple IP
addresses and ports to listen to.

You can also use Port to specify the port Apache listens to, but if a Listen directive is specified, the Port
directive will not have an effect. Please refer to
Chapter 4 for information on how the Port directive
is also used for constructing self-referential URLs.

There is more configuration involved when you need
to support name-based virtual hosts. Please see
Chapter 5 for details.

In addition to Listen, Apache 1.3 provides a related
directive, BindAddress. It is obsolete and its use is dis-
couraged.

Changing the User Apache Runs As

```
User nobody
Group nobody
```

You can specify the user and group Apache runs under
with the User and Group directives. For security reasons, it is not a good idea to run any kind of server as
root because a configuration or programming flaw can
expose the whole server. When Apache is run as root,
it will perform all the actions that require superuser
privileges (such as binding to port 80) and then it will
serve the actual requests as the user and group specified in the Apache configuration. This user ID will
typically have reduced privileges and capabilities.

Specifying a Server Name

```
ServerName www.example.com
```

Sometimes Apache needs to construct self-referential URLs. That is, it needs to construct a URL that refers to the server itself. For example, it may need to redirect a request to a different page or print the website address at the end of a generated error page. By default, this is done using the domain specified with the ServerName directive. Please see Chapter 2 for details on how to use UseCanonicalName and Port to control this behavior.

If no server name is present, Apache will try to infer a valid server name by performing a reverse DNS lookup on the server's IP address. If the DNS server is not properly set up, this can take a long time and the requester may have to wait through a rather long pause.

Providing an Icon for my Web Page

```
AliasMatch /favicon.ico
/usr/local/apache2/icons/site.ico
```

Many modern browsers, such as Internet Explorer, Mozilla, and Konqueror, enable you to associate an icon with a bookmark. When you bookmark a page, the browser sends a request for a favicon.ico file to the same directory containing the bookmarked document. The favicon.ico file is an icon in the Windows icon format.

You can use the AliasMatch directive to redirect all requests for a favicon.ico to a single location containing the icon for your site, as shown in this example.

Discovering the Modules Available on the Server

```
# httpd -l
```

This command lists the compiled-in modules in your server binary and should return something similar to the following:

```
Compiled in modules:
  core.c
  prefork.c
  http_core.c
  mod_so.c
```

If you compiled Apache with loadable module support, your modules will be built as shared-libraries and placed by default in a directory named modules/ (Apache 2.x) or libexec/ (Apache 1.3). To take a look at what shared modules are loaded into the server at runtime, you will need to take a look at the httpd.conf file and look for the appropriate LoadModule directives. With Apache 2.1/2.2, this is not necessary, as httpd -M will list all modules including those loaded at runtime.

Enabling and Disabling Individual Modules

```
./configure (...) --enable-status
./configure (...) --disable-status
```

You can enable/disable individual modules at compile time using the --enable-*module* and --disable-*module* options of the configure command. The preceding example explains how to do so for the mod_status module distributed as part of Apache.

If your server has been compiled with loadable module support, you can disable a module by simply commenting the line that loads the module in the server:

```
#LoadModule mod_status modules/mod_status.so
```

In Apache 1.3, you can clear the list of active modules, including those compiled-in, using a ClearModuleList directive. In that case, you will need to use an AddModule directive for each module you want to use. The functionality provided by ClearModuleList is not available in Apache 2.x

If you disable a module, make sure you remove it from your htttp.conf file directives provided by that module or include them inside a <ifModule> section as shown. Otherwise, the server may fail to start.

```
<ifModule mod_status.c>
  ExtendedStatus On
</ifModule>
```

Adding Modules after Compiling Apache Without Recompiling

```
# apxs -cia mod_usertrack.c
```

Yes, you can add modules to Apache without recompiling, but only if mod_so is already compiled into your server. To find out whether mod_so is compiled into your Apache installation, please read the earlier section, "Discovering the Modules Available on the Server."

You can build a module from sources using apxs, which is a tool for building and installing extension modules that is included by default with Apache.

To compile and install a module with apxs, you just need to change your current directory to the one containing the module and type the following:

```
# apxs -c mod_usertrack.c
```

This will compile the module. You will need now to copy the module to the Apache modules directory and edit the configuration file. You can let apxs automatically handle all this with

```
# apxs -cia mod_usertrack.c
```

This approach will work for simple modules, such as those included with the Apache distribution. For complex third-party modules, such as PHP or mod_python, there is usually a --with-apxs or --with-apxs2 switch to pass to the configure script.

If you have a binary version of the module available, you don't need to do any of these apxs-related steps.

This may be the case if you already compiled many of the optional modules when building the server or the module is already provided as part of your Linux distribution or Windows installation package.

If you are using Apache 1.3, you can add the new module to the server by editing your httpd.conf file and adding the following lines:

```
LoadModule usertrack_module libexec/mod_usertrack.so
AddModule mod_usertrack.c
```

If you are using Apache 2.2, you will only need to add the LoadModule directive, in this case using modules/ instead of libexec/ as the directory where the loadable modules are installed by default.

Publishing Content

```
DocumentRoot /usr/local/apache/htdocs
```

By default, Apache serves content from the htdocs/ directory (which historically stands for HTML documents) in the installation directory. You can place documents there and they will automatically appear in the URL space of the document. For example, if you create a directory inside htdocs named foo and place the file bar.html inside it, it will be accessible from the outside as

```
http://www.example.com/foo/bar.html
```

You can change the location for the documents directory with the DocumentRoot directive, as shown. If a relative path is specified then it will be considered relative to the path specified by the ServerRoot directive.

You don't necessarily need to place your content under the document root directory. One of the strengths of Apache is that it provides a number of powerful and flexible mechanisms for mapping URLs requested by clients into files on disks or resources provided by modules. Please see Chapter 4 for details.

Directive Containers

Directive containers, also called sections, limit the scope to which directives apply. If directives are not inside a container, they belong to the default server scope (server config), applying to the server as a whole.

```
<Directory "/usr/local/apache/htdocs">
...
</Directory>
<Location "/downloads/*.html">
...
</Location>
<FilesMatch "\.(gif|jpg)">
...
</FilesMatch>
```

Default Apache Directive Containers

The following directive containers are the default containers used in Apache configuration files.

<VirtualHost>—A VirtualHost directive specifies a virtual server. Apache enables you to host different websites with a single Apache installation, as described in Chapter 5.

<Directory> and <DirectoryMatch>—These containers apply directives to a certain directory or group of

directories in the file system. The DirectoryMatch container allows regular expression patterns to be used as arguments.

<Location> and <LocationMatch>—Applies directives to certain requested URLs or URL patterns. They are similar to Directory containers.

<Files> and <FilesMatch>—Similar to Directory and Location containers, Files sections apply directives to certain files or file patterns.

These are not the only directive containers available. Modules, such as mod_proxy, may provide their own containers, as explained in Chapter 10. See also Chapter 8 for details on containers that limit access based on HTTP methods.

NOTE: Directory, Files, and Location sections can also take regular expression arguments by preceding them with a ~. Regular expressions are strings that describe or match a set of strings, according to certain syntax rules. For example, the following regular expression will match all requests asking for an image file with a .jpg or .gif extension: <Files ~ "\.(gif|jpg)">. However, the DirectoryMatch, LocationMatch, and FilesMatch directives are preferred for clarity. You can learn more about regular expressions at http://en.wikipedia.org/wiki/Regular_expression.

Directive Containers for Conditional Evaluation

Apache provides support for conditional containers. Directives enclosed in these containers will be processed only if certain conditions are met.

<IfDefine>—Directives in this container will be processed if a specific command-line switch is passed to the Apache executable. In the following example, the command-line switch should be -DSSL. Similarly, you can negate the argument with a "!", as in <IfDefine !SSL>, if you want the directives to apply if the switch was not passed.

<IfModule>—Directives in an IfModule section will be processed only if the module passed as an argument is present in the web server. The default Apache configuration file includes such examples for different MPMs modules.

For example, in the httpd.conf file, you would see

```
<IfDefine SSL>
LoadModule ssl_module modules/mod_ssl.so
</IfDefine>
```

And you would enable it at the command line like this:

```
# httpd -DSSL
```

## 2

Troubleshooting

This chapter covers in detail the most common issues found when running Apache, such as problems with file permissions and not being able to bind to a certain port, and how to fix them. It also explains several tools and resources available to isolate the cause of most problems.

Help! My Apache Server Does Not Work!

We know there is nothing more frustrating than not been able to keep reading a technical book because you cannot get the software to work. We don't want to be one of those books! Hence the reason to address this topic early on. Because of that, this chapter covers both basic and advanced topics, so feel free to skip the ones that do not apply to you if you are new to Apache.

The Error Log

```
ErrorLog logs/error_log
```

The error log file keeps track of important events in the life of the server, including starts, restarts, warnings or errors related to the operation of the server, and forbidden or invalid requests. This is the first place to look when you are trying to solve a problem with the server.

On Unix systems, the error_log file is placed by default in the logs/ directory of your Apache installation. If you are using an installation of Apache that came with your distribution, this file may be in a different location, most commonly /var/log/httpd.

On Windows, the file is named error.log and placed under the logs directory as well.

Use the ErrorLog directive to specify the path to the error log file. Prefix the path to the program with a pipe to log errors to the standard input of another program. This common technique is described in detail in Chapter 3.

Note that the error file will not be created until the first time you start Apache!

Logging to the System Log Daemon

```
ErrorLog syslog
ErrorLog syslog:local7
```

On Unix systems, specify `syslog` as the argument to
`ErrorLog` to instruct Apache to use the system log
daemon to log Apache errors. This is shown in the
example. You can optionally attach a facility (by default
`local7`) as shown. A syslog facility is an information
field that is associated with a syslog message to indicate
the source of a log message. Facilities local0 to local10
are reserved for use by administrators and applications,
such as Apache.

Controlling the Amount of Information Logged

```
LogLevel notice
```

The error information provided by Apache can be cat-
egorized according to degrees of importance. Use the
`LogLevel` directive, supplying one of the arguments
shown in Table 2.1, to choose the messages that you
want to receive. Only errors of that level of importance or higher will be logged.

The default error level of "warn" is appropriate for
most Apache installations. If you are trying to troubleshoot a specific configuration, however, you can
lower the level all the way to "debug" to get much
more detailed logging information.

Table 2.1   LogLevel Options As Described in the Apache Documentation

Setting	Description	Example
emerg	Emergencies—system is unusable	Child cannot open lock file. Exiting.
alert	Action must be taken immediately	getpwuid: couldn't determine user name from uid.
crit	Critical conditions	socket: Failed to get a socket, exiting child.
error	Error conditions	Premature end of script headers.
warn	Warning conditions	Child process 1234 did not exit, sending another SIGHUP.
notice	Normal but significant condition	httpd: caught SIGBUS, attempting to dump core in...
info	Informational	Server seems busy, (You may need to increase StartServers, or Min/MaxSpareServers)...
debug	Debug-level messages	Opening config file...

Testing the Apache Configuration for Problems

```
# apachectl configtest
```

Use this command to test the Apache configuration file for common problems before you use it with a live server. Apache uses the same process to test your configuration each time you issue a restart command using apachectl. This guarantees that a running server will be able to restart successfully using the new configuration file.

Testing Apache from the Command Line

```
$ telnet www.apache.org 80
Trying 192.87.106.226...
Connected to ajax-1.apache.org (192.87.106.226).
Escape character is '^]'.
HEAD / HTTP/1.0

HTTP/1.1 200 OK
Date: Sun, 04 Sep 2005 20:42:02 GMT
Server: Apache/2.0.54 (Unix) mod_ssl/2.0.54
    OpenSSL/0.9.7a DAV/2 SVN/1.2.0-dev
Last-Modified: Sat, 03 Sep 2005 11:35:42 GMT
ETag: "203a8-2de2-3ffdc7a6d3f80"
Accept-Ranges: bytes
Content-Length: 11746
Cache-Control: max-age=86400
Expires: Mon, 05 Sep 2005 20:42:02 GMT
Connection: close
Content-Type: text/html; charset=ISO-8859-1
Connection closed by foreign host.
```

Because HTTP is a simple text-based protocol, you can use a telnet client, a program that allows you to connect directly to a server and port you specify, to test for the presence of a working Apache server from the command line. If you receive no response to a remote telnet request and are positive that your network is properly configured, Apache is not listening on the address and port in question. This can be useful for troubleshooting in environments where a web browser is not available, as can be the case when accessing a server remotely over SSH. For example, if you can access Apache in a remote machine from the `localhost` address using telnet, but not remotely using a browser, it may indicate firewall problems or an incorrect setting of the Apache `Listen` directive.

Connect via telnet to www.apache.org (or your favorite website) at port 80 and type

```
HEAD / HTTP/1.0
```

or

```
GET / HTTP/1.0
```

Press the Enter key twice. You will get a response similar to the example.

If you have the lynx command-line browser installed in your Unix system, you can get a similar result by issuing the command

```
lynx -head  -dump http://www.apache.org
```

Chapter 7 covers `mod_ssl` and explains a similar way to connect to an SSL-enabled web server using the `openssl` command-line tool.

Checking That Apache Is Running

```
ps -aux | grep httpd
25297 ?          S       0:00 /usr/local/www/bin/
    httpd -k start
15874 ?          S       0:06 /usr/local/www/bin
    /httpd -k start
14441 ?          S       0:02 /usr/local/www/bin
    /httpd -k start
...
/usr/sbin/lsof | grep httpd |grep IPv
httpd     14441     nobody    3u  IPv4      136524
                    TCP www.example.com:http (LISTEN)
httpd     25297     root      3u  IPv4      136524
                    TCP www.example.com:http (LISTEN)
httpd     30277     nobody    3u  IPv4      136524
                    TCP www.example.com:http (LISTEN)
...
netstat -ltnp
Active Internet connections (only servers)
Proto Recv-Q Send-Q Local Address              Foreign
    Address              State        PID/Program name
tcp        0      0 192.168.1.151:80            0.0.0.0:
    *                    LISTEN       25297/httpd
tcp        0      0 0.0.0.0:22                  0.0.0.0:
    *                    LISTEN       1038/sshd
```

Sometimes, you may not be able to connect to the server and are therefore unsure of whether the server is running or there is a network problem. In Unix systems, you can use a number of command-line tools to help you find out. The example shows some of them.

The `ps` tool shows whether or not the `httpd` process is running on the system.

The `netstat` and `lsof` tools show the port and address on which the Apache server is listening.

In Windows systems, you can use the Windows task
manager (invoked by pressing Ctrl-Alt-Del) to see
whether the Apache.exe process is running.
Alternatively, you can use the Apache monitor tray
application included with recent distributions to check
the status of Apache.

Alternate Ways of Stopping Apache

```
# kill -HUP 25297
# kill -9 25297
```

Sometimes it is necessary or convenient to signal the
server directly using the `kill` command-line utility
instead of the `apachectl` wrapper script. To do this, first
find the process id of the running Apache server using
`ps` or `lsof` as shown . Then, end the process with the
`kill` command-line tool, supplying the signal to be
sent as the first argument and the Apache server's
process id (25297 in this example) as the second argument. Use `HUP` as the signal to stop the server or `SIGHUP`
as the signal to restart the server. You can also replace
the signal with its numerical equivalent, as shown in
the example. Read the `kill` manual page for details.

In Linux, you can send a signal to all processes named
`httpd` with the `killall` command. For example, you
can kill all `httpd` processes using

```
# killall -HUP httpd
```

You need to be careful, because if you are running several Apache instances, this command will take them all
down!

Note that you need to have the appropriate permissions for these commands to work. In nearly all cases, you must either be the superuser or the owner of the Apache process in order to end or restart it.

In Windows systems, you can force Apache to stop by using the Windows Task Manager and pressing the End Task button.

Using Apache to Debug Apache

There are number of Apache modules that can help you when troubleshooting or debugging an Apache setup or a web application.

mod_loopback, a Web client debugging tool, simply echoes back to the browser everything received concerning an HTTP request, including POST or PUT data.

```
http://www.snert.com/Software/mod_loopback/index.
shtml
```

mod_tee and mod_trace_output are third-party modules that store the content as it is being served. They can be found at these URLs:

```
http://apache.webthing.com/mod_tee/
http://trace-output.sourceforge.net/
```

mod_logio, distributed with Apache 2, dumps all data received or returned by the server into the error log for debugging purposes.

All of these modules have an effect on performance, but can be very useful when debugging, for example, header or cookie-related issues.

Startup Errors

This section explains a number of problems that may prevent Apache from starting and the error that you will receive for each.

Syntax Error

```
Syntax error on line xxx of /etc/httpd/httpd.conf:
```

Invalid command 'PiidFile', perhaps misspelled or defined by a module not included in the server configuration

A syntax error indicates that you have misspelled a directive (in this case, PidFile) in the configuration file or that you have included one or more directives used by a module that has not been added to the server. Check the syntax of the configuration file indicated in the error message. See Chapter 1 for details on using an <ifModule> directive to conditionally exclude directives so that the configuration file can still be processed when a module is not available.

Address Already in Use

```
"Address already in use: make_sock: could not bind
to port"
```

An address already in use error means that another program is using the port Apache is trying to bind to. To solve the problem, either stop the program that is using that port before starting Apache, or edit the httpd.conf configuration file and change the port on which Apache will listen for requests by adjusting the values given after the Listen and Port directives.

In most cases an address already in use error happens because another Apache server is already running on your system or, in the case of Windows, an Internet Information Server or Microsoft Personal Web Server instance is running on the port Apache has been configured to use. Other popular programs, such as Skype, are also known to use port 80 on certain occasions.

Could Not Bind to Port

```
[Mon Jan 9 20:09:50 2005] [crit] (13)Permission
denied: make_sock: could not bind to port 80
```

A could not bind to port error indicates that you do not have the necessary permissions to request that Apache bind to the port specified in the Apache configuration file. On Unix, only privileged users can bind to ports between 1 and 1024. To solve this problem, log in as root or issue the su command and try to start the server again. If you do not have root access, edit your httpd.conf file and change the port that Apache uses to a number greater than 1024.

Module Not Compatible

```
"module xxx is not compatible with this version of
Apache"
```

A module not compatible error occurs when Apache tries to load a module that was compiled for a newer (or older) Apache server than the one currently installed. If you have the source code for the module, you may be able to recompile it using your current Apache installation, as shown in Chapter 1. If you do not have source code for or are unable to recompile a module whose functionality is essential to you, upgrade (or downgrade) your Apache server to a version compatible with the module.

Name Resolution

> "Cannot determine hostname"

Several Apache directives, including ServerName and Listen, accept hostnames as arguments. However, if Apache is not able to resolve a supplied hostname to an IP address at startup time using the Domain Name Service (DNS) or your system's host list, you will receive the cannot determine hostname error. To solve the problem, verify your DNS and /etc/hosts settings and the spellings of hostnames supplied in httpd.conf. Whenever possible, use IP addresses for directives such as Listen and <VirtualHost> instead of hostnames.

Cannot Open Log or Configuration File

> (13)Permission denied: httpd: could not open error log file /usr/local/apache/logs/error_log.

A permission denied error indicates that you do not have sufficient permissions either to read the Apache configuration file(s) or to write to the Apache log files.

This problem often happens when Apache is launched by a different user than the one who built and installed it. Either start Apache as superuser or as the user that installed it, or, if you have sufficient permission to do so, use chmod to change ownership of the file named in the error message.

Access Denied Errors

"Forbidden/You don't have permission to access /xxx on this server"

If your web browser returns 403 Forbidden/Access Denied when you attempt to load a web page through your Apache server, it means that the requested URL is subject to access restrictions that were not met by your request. To solve this problem, change the permissions of the web content or files that you have requested, and ensure that all directories leading to the document in question are both read- and execute-accessible to the owner of the Apache process. In Unix systems, you can use the chmod utility to set those permissions.

A "Client denied by server configuration" statement in the error log indicates that the denial results from access control directives (such as Allow and Deny) in the <Directory> or <Location> sections for that URL in your Apache configuration files.

A "Directory index forbidden by rule" statement in the error log indicates that you have attempted to view a directory in which no index file can be found. For details on directory indexing and index files, read about the Indexes option of the Options directive, covered in Chapter 6.

Options ExecCGI is off in this directory

If when attempting to execute a CGI-script you see "Options ExecCGI is off in this directory," it means that you have not marked the CGI as executable in the Apache configuration file or that CGI scripts cannot be run from the directory in question. Read about the ScriptAlias or Options directive for more information.

Internal Server Errors

Internal server errors are errors that prevent Apache from fulfilling a request.

Segmentation Faults

```
"child pid xxx exit signal Segmentation Fault (11)"
```

A segmentation fault occurs when the Apache server attempts to access memory areas belonging to other system processes or a malformed or illegal instruction is encountered by the system in the Apache process. This is caused either by a bug, usually in poorly written or experimental libraries or modules, or by hardware faults, usually in the system memory, chipset, bus, or processor.

Premature End of Script Headers

```
[error] [client 192.168.200.3] Premature end of
script headers: /usr/local/apache/cgi-bin/test-cgi
```

A premature end of script headers error is caused by incomplete CGI script execution. Make sure the CGI program has executable permissions and that the interpreter in the first line of the script points to the correct program. For example, you will receive this error if your script begins with #!/usr/local/bin/perl on its first line when in reality your Perl interpreter is located at /usr/bin/perl.

"Premature end of headers" errors are generally due to abnormal program termination before the script has returned any data. Program failures can be caused by a variety of additional reasons, including errors in your code or missing libraries to which the program is linked. In some cases, the operating system or Apache might terminate the process if its resource usage (memory, CPU time) exceeds a certain limit, as explained in Chapter 9.

Malformed Headers

```
[error] [client 192.168.200.3] malformed header from
script. Bad header=xxx: /usr/local/apache/cgi-bin/
example.cgi
```

A malformed header from script error occurs when headers are not in the appropriate format (usually because of a programming error). The Apache server expects the response from the script to start with zero or more headers, followed by an empty line.

Additional Error Log Files

```
RewriteLog /usr/local/apache/logs/rewrite_log
RewriteLogLevel warn
SSLLog /usr/local/apache/logs/ssl_log
SSLLogLevel warn
ScriptLog logs/cgi_log
```

A number of modules, including the Apache 1.3 SSL module, mod_rewrite, and mod_cgi provide their own directive for logging module-specific data to a separate file.

Redirections Do Not Work

```
UseCanonicalName off
```

If your Apache server becomes unreachable whenever the server issues a redirect, it may be because the canonical name of your host is inaccessible from outside your network or incorrect.

For example, a `ServerName` set to localhost, 127.0.0.1, or a private address will be inaccessible if the server redirects the user to a URL based on these values.

To solve this problem, provide a valid `ServerName` or set `UseCanonicalName` to "off" so that self-referential URLs are constructed with the hostname provided by the client. This is a common issue with machines behind a reverse proxy, which is discussed in Chapter 10.

Troubleshooting Checklist

This section summarizes some of the most common issues found when troubleshooting an Apache problem.

Starting the Server

If you cannot successfully start the server, check the error log for information on why the failure occurred.

If another server is already running at that address, choose a different address/port combination for your server.

If you do not have permissions to bind to the requested port, start Apache as the superuser (root) so that you have access to bind to privileged ports.

If Apache is unable to open the configuration or log files, ensure that the files are owned by the same user that installed Apache and that the user in question has permission to write to them.

Connecting to the Server

If you are trying to access a page in the server and it does not display, to solve the problem you must first try to isolate whether it is caused by the server, network, or browser.

First, ensure that Apache is running using `ps`, `netstat`, or the Task Manager (in Windows). It may be that the server is not running at all.

Then ensure that you can connect to Apache from the local machine. To do this, use telnet to connect directly to the server and issue a sample request.

Next, ensure that Apache running on the correct address/port combination. If you can access the server locally, but not remotely, Apache is likely listening on a local address or port that is not accessible remotely. Use `netstat` or `lsof` to determine on which addresses Apache is listening and ensure that they are correct.

Ensure that your firewall or router is correctly configured. If Apache is listening to the correct address but is inaccessible outside your network, network traffic to your Apache server may be blocked. Use the `traceroute` utility (`tracert` on Windows) to test for network connectivity between the hosts in question. Many operating systems prevent access from the outside by default except on a few selected ports. If you are running Apache on a nonstandard port, you may be blocked. How to fix this varies from distribution to distribution. For example, you can use the `system-config-securitylevel` tool on Fedora systems and the Windows Firewall tool in the Windows Control Panel.

Finally, if you are using Secure Sockets Layer (SSL) to access the server (explained in Chapter 7) and you are connecting using older browser versions or running unusual configurations, check the error log for problems related to SSL data encryption.

Document Not Found

If you can access the server, but you get a "Document not found" error, ensure that the document does indeed exist in the file system.

Then, ensure that the request reached the server by checking the access_log file for request(s) from the host in question. If you have multiple Apache instances running simultaneously, it may be that you are connecting to the wrong server.

Next, ensure that your Alias directives point to the right location—that is, to the location your target documents are located. Make sure that you did not misspell or accidentally delete the target directory.

Finally, check for incorrect redirects, including "trailing slashes" and the ServerName issues described earlier in this chapter.

Access Forbidden

If the document exists but you are told that you have been forbidden from accessing it, check for a number of common errors.

Ensure that the owner of the Apache process has permission to read the file.

Ensure that the owner of the Apache process has read and list permissions for all directories in the path leading to the file.

Check to see whether you are trying to access a directory without an index file when directory listings are forbidden in the Apache configuration file.

Verify that the request meets all of the requirements outlined by the access control directives in the Apache configuration file.

If you are trying to access a CGI-script, ensure that it has been given read and execute permissions.

Internal Server Errors

If you get an "Internal server error" in your browser when you try to load a page from the web server, check the Apache `error_log` to try to find the cause. Ask yourself the following questions:

Are you trying to access a CGI program? Does it have the right read and execute permissions? Is the path to the interpreter in the first line of the script correct? Is it marked as a CGI script by a `ScriptAlias` directive or similar?

If All Else Fails

This chapter has discussed only the most common problems faced by Apache users. If you encounter a problem not covered in this chapter, the first step toward resolving it is to check the error logs for details. Increase the Apache server's `LogLevel`, if necessary, to find hints as to what the problem may be. Search the Apache documentation, mailing lists, and bug database. Finally, post your question to the Apache Users mailing list at the following address, taking care to follow the posting guidelines when doing so: Do your homework first, then provide enough information for others to be able to help.

http://httpd.apache.org/lists.html#http-users

## 3

Logs and Monitoring

Introduction to Logging in Apache

In addition to the error logging functionality described in the previous chapter, Apache provides extensive facilities for recording information about every aspect of a request. This chapter covers the most common issues found when logging requests, such as conditional logging, log rotation, resolution of IP addresses, and piped logging. It also covers a number of bundled and third-party modules and utilities for monitoring the status of your Apache server and to analyze its logs.

Default Apache Log Files

Apache provides a number of monitoring and logging facilities to track the correct operation of the server. The default Apache configuration provides two log files, placed inside the logs directory of the installation directory:

- The access_log file (access.log in Windows) contains information about the requests that have been served by the server, such as the URL requested, the IP address of the client, and whether the request completed successfully or not.

- The error_log file (error.log in Windows) contains information related to error conditions, as well as different events in the lifecycle of the server.

Creating Log Formats

```
LogFormat "%h %l %u %t \"%r\" %>s %b" common
LogFormat "%h %l %u %t \"%r\" %>s %b"
    \"%{Referer}i\" \"%{User-agent}i\"" combined
```

The LogFormat directive allows you to tell Apache which aspects of the request you want to record. You will still need additional directives to tell Apache where to log that information, but that is addressed in the next section. This example shows the configuration for the two most popular formats, the Common Log Format and the Combined Log Format. When Apache receives a request, it will substitute each one of the fields prefixed by a % with the corresponding request attribute. If you are using the CLF, each entry in your log file will look like this:

```
192.168.200.4 - someuser [12/Jun/2005:08:33:34
    +0500] "GET /example.png HTTP/1.0" 200 1234
```

If you are using the combined common format, each entry in your log file will look like this:

```
192.168.200.4 - someuser [12/Jun/2005:08:33:34
    +0500] "GET /example.png HTTP/1.0" 200 1234
    http://www.example.com/index.html "Mozilla/5.0
    (Windows; U; Windows NT 5.1; en-US; rv:1.7.7)"
```

Although the appendix provides a comprehensive logging format reference, this list describes the most important fields:

- %h: The IP address of the client that sent the request to the web server, or the client's hostname if you have HostNameLookups enabled (192.168.200.4 in this example.)

- %u: The user id of the user who sent the request determined by HTTP authentication (someuser in the example). See Chapter 6 for more details on how to configure HTTP-based authentication.

- %t: Time when the request was received by the server.

- %r: Text of the original request line from the client including the HTTP method used, the resource requested, and the HTTP protocol version used by the client's browser ("GET /example.png HTTP/1.0" in the example).

- %>s: The final HTTP request status code that the web server sends back to the client (200 in the example, indicating that the request was completed successfully).

- %b: The size in bytes of the object sent to the client in response to the request excluding the response headers (1234 in the example).

The combined log format extends the common log format with two additional fields. It is defined as

- %{Referer}i: The Referer HTTP request header; that is, the web page that referred to the current document (http://www.example.com/index.html in the example).

- %{User-agent}i: The User-agent HTTP request header. It includes information about the client's browser ("Mozilla/5.0 (Windows; U; Windows NT 5.1; en-US; rv:1.7.7)" in the example).

Creating a Custom Log File

```
CustomLog logs/access_log common
TransferLog logs/sample.log
```

You may want to create new log files in addition to the ones included with Apache. This example uses CustomLog to create a new log file and store the information defined by a previously defined log format named common, as seen in the previous section. You can replace the nickname with the format definition itself. An additional, simpler directive is TransferLog, which will just take the definition provided by the latest LogFormat directive.

Redirecting Logs to an External Program

```
TransferLog "|bin/rotatelogs /var/logs/apachelog
86400"
```

You can also use CustomLog or TransferLog to redirect
("pipe") the log output to an external program instead
of a file. To do this, you need to begin with the pipe
character "|", followed by the path to a program that
will receive the log information on its standard input.
This example uses the rotatelogs program included
with Apache, which is described in a later section.

When an external program is used, it will be run as
the user who started httpd. This will be root if the
server was started by root; be absolutely sure that the
program is secure. Also, when entering a file path on
non-Unix platforms, care should be taken to make
sure that only forward slashes are used, even though
the platform may allow the use of backslashes. In general, it is a good idea to always use forward slashes
throughout the configuration files.

Logging Requests Conditionally

```
SetEnvIf Request_URI "(\.gif|\.jpg)$" image
CustomLog logs/access_log common env=!image

SetEnvIf Remote_Addr  192\.168\.200\.5 specialma-
chine
CustomLog logs/special_access_log common env=spe-
cialmachine
```

You can decide whether or not to log a request based
on the presence of an environment variable. This variable can be previously set based on a number of
parameters, such as the client's IP address or the presence of a certain header in the request. As shown in
this example, the CustomLog directive can accept an
environment variable as a third argument. If the environment variable is present, the entry will be logged;

otherwise, it will not. If the environment variable is negated by prefixing it with an "!", the entry will be logged if the variable is *not* present. The example shows you how to avoid logging images in GIF and JPEG format and how to log requests from a particular IP address to a separate log file. See the next section for another example.

Monitoring Who Is Linking to Your Website

```
SetEnvIfNoCase Referer www\.example\.com internalre-
ferral
LogFormat "%{Referer}i -> %U" referer
CustomLog logs/referer.log referer env=!internalre-
ferral
```

In order to monitor who is linking to your website, you can log the Referer: header from the request. This header contains the URL that linked to the page being requested. While not always present or accurate, it works for the majority of cases. This example shows how to use an environment variable to log the referrer information to a separate file. In this particular case, we are only interested in logging external referers, not those that come from an internal web page. To do so, in this example we check whether the referrer matches our own domain.

Monitoring Apache with mod_status

```
<Location /server-status>
  SetHandler server-status
  Order Deny,Allow
  Deny from all
  Allow from 192.168.0
</Location>
```

The mod_status module provides information on server activity and performance, allowing a server administrator to find out how well their server is performing. An HTML page is presented that gives the current server statistics in an easily readable form, such as the number of workers serving requests, the number of idle workers, the time the server was started/restarted, and so on.

If you include an ExtendedStatus On directive, additional information will be displayed, such as individual information about each worker status, total number of accesses, current requests being processed, and so on.

Bear in mind that, depending on your server load, this extended statistics recording may have a significant impact on server performance.

This example shows how to enable the mod_status monitoring, while restricting access to this information to only certain IP addresses. You can now access server statistics by using a Web browser to access the page at http://www.example.com/server-status.

Monitoring Apache with SNMP

There are a couple of open-source modules that add Simple Network Management Protocol (SNMP) capabilities to the Apache web server. This protocol is commonly used to manage network servers and equipment from a central console such as HP OpenView and Tivoli. With this module, you can easily monitor Apache performance in real time, including server uptime, load average, number of errors in a certain period of time, number of bytes and requests served, and many other metrics. The SNMP modules can also generate alarms when a certain threshold or error condition is met, such as a sudden increase in the number of simultaneous client connections.

For Apache 1.3, you can use mod_snmp, which can be found at http://www.mod-snmp.com/ and supports SNMP version 1 and 2. It requires patching of the Apache core.

For Apache 2, you can use a similar module called mod_apache_snmp. It can be found at http://mod-apache-snmp.sourceforge.net/. This module supports versions 1, 2, and 3 of the SNMP protocol and can be compiled as a DSO, without the need to patch Apache.

A number of open-source tools and frameworks allow you to manage SNMP resources, such as the tools at http://www.net-snmp.org, OpenNMS (http://www.opennms.org), and Nagios (http://www.nagios.org).

Analyzing Your Logs with Open-source Tools

There are a number of commercial and open-source tools that you can use to process and display your log data. They usually take a log file, analyze its contents, and create a series of web pages with the relevant statistics.

The following are some popular, freely available, open source applications for general log analysis:

- Webalizer—http://www.mrunix.net/webalizer/
- AWStats—http://awstats.sf.net

Other tools allow you more advanced log processing, such as visually displaying the path followed by your visitors:

- Visitors—http://www.hping.org/visitors/
- Pathalizer—http://pathalizer.bzzt.net/

Monitoring Your Logs in Real Time

In addition to mod_status and the various SNMP modules described earlier, you can use the apachetop command-line tool, which can be downloaded from http://clueful.shagged.org/apachetop/.

This tool works similarly to the Unix top command-line tool, but instead of displaying the status of the operating system, it displays the status of the web server in real time.

If you run Apache on a Unix system and you have a website with low traffic, you can use the `tail` command-line utility to rudimentarily monitor, in real time, log entries both to your access and error logs:

```
tail -f logfile
```

There are additional programs that enable you to quickly identify problems by scanning your error log files for specific errors, malformed requests, and so on, and reporting on them:

- Logscan can be found at http://www.garand.net/security.php
- ScanErrLog can be found at http://www.librelogiciel.com/software/

Logging Requests to a Database

Apache itself does not include tools for logging to databases, but a few third-party scripts and modules are available:

- `mod_log_sql` allows you to log requests directly to a MySQL database: http://www.outoforder.cc/projects/apache/mod_log_sql/
- You can then query the database using the Apache LogView SQL tool: http://freshmeat.net/projects/apachelogviewsql/
- `pglogd` collects logs and stores log entries in a PostgreSQL database: http://www.digitalstratum.com/pglogd/.

Rotating and Archiving Logs

```
CustomLog "|bin/rotatelogs /var/logs/apachelog
86400" common
```

If you have a website with high traffic, your log files will quickly grow in size. While you can always archive the log files by hand, there are a number of mechanisms to rotate logs periodically, archiving and compressing older logs at well-defined intervals.

To avoid having to stop or restart the server when manipulating the log files, a common solution is to use an intermediate program to log the requests. The program will in turn take care of rotating, compressing, and archiving the logs.

Apache provides the `rotatelogs` tool for this purpose. You can find a similar, alternative program at http://cronolog.org/.

This example uses the `rotatelogs` tool to create a new log file and move the current log to the `/var/logs` directory daily (86400 is the number of seconds in one day). Check the Apache documentation for details on how to use `rotatelogs` to also rotate logs based on size and name archived files based on a template.

CAUTION: If the path to the log rotation program includes spaces, you might need to escape them by prefixing them with a \ (backslash). This is especially common in the Windows platform.

Controlling IP Address Resolution

```
HostNameLookups on
```

If you set the HostNameLookups directive to on then Apache will try to determine (resolve) the hostname corresponding to the client's IP-address when it logs the request.

With HostNameLookups set to off, an access_log entry may look like

```
192.168.200.4 - someuser [12/Jun/2005:08:33:34
    +0500] "GET /example.png HTTP/1.0" 200 1234
```

And with HostNameLookups set to on, the same entry would look like

```
unit12.example.com - someuser [12/Jun/2005:08:33:34
    +0500] "GET /example.png HTTP/1.0" 200 1234
```

The next section explains the reverse process, how to replace IP addresses in logs with hostnames.

Processing Logged IP Addresses

```
$ logresolve < access_log > resolved_log
```

Setting HostNameLookups to on can have an impact on the server's performance, slowing its response time. To avoid using this directive setting, it is possible to disable name resolution and use a separate post-processing utility that can scan the log files and replace the IP addresses with host names. These tools are more efficient because they can cache results and they do not cause any delay when serving requests to clients.

Apache includes one such tool, logresolve (logre-solve.exe in Windows). It reads log entries from standard input and outputs the result to its standard output. To read to and from a file, you can use redirection, on both Unix and Windows, as shown in the example.

You should bear in mind that the result of an IP address resolution result will not always correspond to the real hostname that sent the request. For example, if there is a proxy or gateway between the client and the web server, the IP address reported by HostNameLookups or logresolve will be the IP address of the proxy or gateway and you will get the hostname of the proxy server or the IP block managed by the gateway, rather than the name of an actual host.

Restarting Apache Automatically If It Fails

```
#!/bin/bash
if [ `ps -waux | grep -v grep | grep -c httpd` -lt 1
]; then apachectl restart; fi
```

If you install Apache on Windows as a service, it can be automatically restarted by the service manager if it crashes.

In Unix, you can implement this functionality with a watchdog script. A watchdog monitors the status of another program, and if the program crashes or stops for any reason, the watchdog starts it again. The example shows a simple Linux script that will monitor the system process list to ensure that an httpd process exists, and will restart httpd if it crashes. To use it, you will need to give it executable permissions and add it to your `cron` configuration so it can be run at predefined intervals.

If you are running Solaris, use `ps -ef` instead of `ps -waux`.

You can find a more sophisticated watchdog script that will send email when the server is down, and can watch specific `httpd` process ids, at the following URL: http://perl.apache.org/docs/general/control/control.html.

Most Linux distributions also include their own generic watchdog scripts that can be adapted to work with Apache.

Merging and Splitting Log Files

When you have a cluster of web servers serving the same content, it is often necessary to merge logs from all servers into a unique log file before passing it to analysis tools. Similarly, if a single Apache server handles several virtual hosts, sometimes it is necessary to split a single log file into different files, one per each virtual host. This can be done at the web server level, as explained in the next section, or by post-processing the log file. Both Apache 1.3 and 2.x come with a support script file named `split-logfile`. It can be found in the `support/` directory of the Apache source distribution.

The logtool project provides a collection of log manipulation tools, and can be found at http://www.coker.com.au/logtools/.

The `vlogger` tool allows splitting a single log stream into several virtualhost-specific log files, as well as being able to replace tools such as `cronolog`, as explained in a previous section. It can be found at http://n0rp.chemlab.org/vlogger/.

Keeping Separate Logs for Each Virtual Host

```
<VirtualHost 192.168.200.3>
ServerName vhost1.example.com
CustomLog logs/vhost1.example.com_log combined
ErrorLog logs/vhost2.example.com_log
.......
</Virtual Host>
```

You can keep separate access logs for each virtual host using a `CustomLog` directive inside each `<VirtualHost>` section, as shown in the example.

You can also choose to log the operations of all virtual hosts in the `access_log` defined in the global server context:

```
LogFormat "%v %h %l %u %t \"%r\" %>s %b" common_vir-
tualhost
CustomLog logs/access_log common_virtualhost
```

`%v` will log the name of the virtual host that serves the request. You can then use the tools described in the previous section to process the resulting log file. This may be necessary if you have a large number of virtual hosts.

If you don't want to keep track of the operations of a particular host at all, you can simply use

```
CustomLog /dev/null
```

Common Log Entries

In addition to the information provided in Chapter 2, this section describes a number of log entries for some common errors that you may find when you review your log files. You can safely ignore most of them.

File favicon.ico Not Found

Most recent web browsers support displaying a custom icon next to the browser's location bar or when storing a bookmark. To do so, the browser requests a specific file from the website (favicon.ico). If this file is not present, you will get this error. You can learn more about how to provide this icon in your website in Chapter 1.

File robots.txt Not Found

The robots.txt file is a file requested by certain programs, such as automatic downloaders and web crawlers, when accessing your website. These are programs that scan websites, recursively following and downloading any links that they find. They are usually associated with search engines, and their main purpose is to store and index the retrieved contents. If the robots.txt file is not present, you will get this error.

httpd.pid Overwritten

On Unix systems, the httpd.pid file contains the PID (process id) for the Apache process currently running. It is created when Apache starts and deleted when it shuts down. When Apache does not have a clean shutdown, for example because the server had to be killed manually or the machine crashed, the file will not be deleted. In this case, it will still be present the next time the server starts, giving this error.

Long, Strange Requests

You may find strange requests such as the following in your error log:

```
"SEARCH /\x90\x02\xb1\x02\xb1\x02\xb1\x02 ..."
"GET /scripts/..%252f../winnt/system32/cmd.exe?/
c+dir HTTP/1.0..."
"GET /default.ida?NNNNNNN NNNNNNNNNNNNNNNNNN ..."
```

Or requests for executable files that do not exist in your website, such as cmd.exe, root.exe, dir, and so on.

There are log entries that result from automated attempts to exploit vulnerabilities in web servers. Luckily, most of them are generated by worms or other malicious applications specific to Microsoft Internet Information Server on Windows, and Apache is not affected. However, from time to time, flaws are discovered in Apache that could leave it vulnerable to remote attacks. For this reason, you should always keep your Apache server up to date, as described in Chapter 6.

4

URL Mapping and Dynamic Content

URL Mapping

This chapter explains how to configure Apache to map requests to files and directories or redirect them to specific pages or servers. This knowledge comes in handy to solve common problems such as maintaining working URLs when the site structure changes, dealing with case-sensitive websites, supporting multiple languages, and so on. It also explains how to use the CGI and server side include functionality present in Apache to provide dynamically generated content.

Mapping URLs to Files with Alias

```
Alias /icons/ /usr/local/apache2/icons/
```

The structure of your website does not need to match the layout of your files on disk. You can use the Alias directive to map directories on disk to specific URLs. For example, this directive will cause a request for http://www.example.com/icons/image.gif to make Apache look for the file in /usr/local/apache2/icons/image.gif instead of under the default document root, in /usr/local/apache2/htdocs/icons/image.gif.

The trailing slashes in the Alias directive are significant. If you include them, the client request must include the slash as well or the Alias directive won't take effect. For example, if you use the following directive

```
Alias /icons/ /usr/local/apache2/icons/
```

and request http://www.example.com/icons, the server will return a 404 Document Not Found error response.

Mapping URL Patterns to Files with AliasMatch

```
AliasMatch ^/(docs|help) /usr/local/apache/htdocs/
manual
```

The AliasMatch directive provides a similar behavior to Alias, but enables you to specify a regular expression for the URL. The matches can be substituted in the destination path. For example, this directive will match any URL under /help or /docs to filesystem paths under the manual directory. Regular expressions are strings that describe or match a set of strings, according to certain syntax rules. You can learn more about regular expressions at http://en.wikipedia.org/wiki/Regular_expression.

Redirecting a Page to Another Location

```
Redirect /news http://news.example.com
Redirect /latest /3.0
```

The structure of a typical website changes over time, and you can't control how other sites link to you, such as search engines with stale links. To avoid errors when people access your website through old links, you can configure Apache with the Redirect directive to redirect those requests to the correct resource, whether it is in the current server or a different one. Although the Redirect directive can take optional arguments indicating the type of redirect (such as temporary or permanent), the most commonly used syntax is to provide an origin URL and a destination URL. The destination URL can be in the same web server or can point to a different web server altogether. In this example, a request for http://www.example.com/news/today/index.html will be redirected to http://news.example.com/today/index.html.

Redirecting to the Latest Version of a File

```
RedirectMatch myapp-(1|2)\.([0-9])(\.[0-9])?-(.*)
/myapp-3.0-$4
```

The RedirectMatch directive is similar to Redirect, but allows the origin URL path to be a regular expression. This allows a great amount of flexibility. For example, imagine you are a software company distributing

downloads from your website and release new versions
of a particular product over time. You may find that a
certain percentage of your users are still downloading
older versions of your software through third-party
websites that have not yet updated their links. Using
`RedirectMatch`, users who request old versions of the
file can be easily redirected to the latest version. For
example, suppose the name of the latest version of
your downloadable file is myapp-3.0. This example will
redirect requests for `http://www.example.com/`
`myapp-2.5.1-demo.tgz` to `http://www.example.com/`
`myapp-3.0-demo.tgz` and requests for `http://`
`www.example.com/myapp-1.2-manual.pdf` to `http://`
`www.example.com/myapp-3.0-manual.pdf`.

The first three elements of the regular expression will
match a major and minor number and an optional
patch number. Those will be replaced by 3.0. The
remaining part of the filename is captured in the final
regular expression group and replaced in the destination URL.

Redirecting Failed or Unauthorized Requests

```
ErrorDocument 404 /search.html
```

If you maintain a popular or complex website, no mat-
ter how careful you are, you will receive a number of
requests for invalid URLs or documents that no longer
exist. Though many of them can be addressed with
proper use of `Redirect`s, there will always be a number
of requests that end up with the dreaded 404
Document Not Found response. For that reason, it

may be desirable to replace the default Apache error page and direct your users to a special location in your website. For example, a page that can help your visitors find the resource they were looking for, such as a search page or site map, as shown in the example. On a related note, Chapter 6 provides additional information on customizing access denied pages.

Defining Content Handlers

```
AddHandler cgi-script .pl .cgi
<Location "/cgi-bin/*.pl">
Options +ExecCGI
SetHandler cgi-script
</Location>
```

Handlers are a way Apache determines which actions to perform on the requested content. Modules provide handlers, and you configure Apache to associate certain content with specific handlers. This functionality is commonly used with content-generation modules such as PHP and mod_cgi. The example shows how to associate the cgi-handler handler with the files you want to run as CGIs.

The AddHandler directive associates a certain handler with filename extensions. RemoveHandler can be used to remove previous associations. In the example, AddHandler tells Apache to treat all documents with cgi or pl extensions as CGI scripts.

The SetHandler directive enables you to associate a handler with all files in a particular directory or location. The Action directive, described later in this chapter, enables you to associate a particular MIME type or handler with a CGI script.

Understanding MIME Types

MIME (Multipurpose Internet Mail Extensions) is a set of standards that defines, among other things, a way to indicate the content type of a document. Examples of MIME types are text/html and audio/mpeg. The first component of the MIME type is the main category of the content (text, audio, image, video) and the second component is the specific type.

Apache uses MIME types to determine which modules or filters will process certain content, and to add HTTP headers to the response to identify its content type. These headers will be used by the client application to identify and correctly display the contents to the end user.

Configuring MIME Types

```
AddType text/xml .xml .schema
<Location /xml-schemas/>
ForceType text/xml
</Location>
```

As with content handlers, you can associate MIME types with specific file extensions or URLs. This example shows how to associate the text/xml MIME type with files ending in .xml and .schema and with all the content under the /xml-schemas/ URL. By default, Apache bundles a mime.types file that includes the most common MIME types and their associated extensions.

Basics of Running CGI Scripts

CGI stands for *Common Gateway Interface*. It is a standard protocol used by web servers to communicate with external programs. The web server provides all the necessary information about the request to an external program, which processes it and returns a response. The response is then transmitted back to the client. CGIs were the original mechanism to generate unique content for every request on-the-fly ("dynamic content") and are supported by nearly every web server. Apache provides support for CGIs using the mod_cgi Apache module (mod_cgid when running a threaded Apache server).

Poorly written or sample CGI programs can be a security risk, so if you are not using this functionality, you may want to disable it altogether, as described in Chapter 6.

Marking Resources As Executable CGIs

```
ScriptAlias /cgi-bin/ /usr/local/apache2/cgi-bin
```

This section shows a number of ways to tell Apache that the target file for a particular request is a CGI script. This is necessary so Apache will not serve the contents of the file directly to the client, but rather return the results of executing it.

The ScriptAlias directive is similar to the Alias directive described earlier in this chapter, but with the difference that Apache will treat every file in the target directory as a CGI script. Alternatively, you can use any <Files>, <Location>, and <Directory> sections in combination with the SetHandler directive to tell Apache that the contents of these sections are CGI programs. In this case, you will also need to provide an Options +ExecCGI directive to tell Apache that CGI execution is allowed. The following example tells Apache to treat all URLs ending with a .pl file extension as CGI scripts.

```
<Location "/cgi-bin/*.pl">
Options +ExecCGI
SetHandler cgi-script
</Location>
```

Associating Scripts with HTTP Methods and MIME Types

```
# Processing all GIF images through a CGI script
# before serving them
Action image/gif /cgi-bin/filter.cgi
# Associating specific HTTP methods with a CGI
# script
Script PUT /cgi-bin/upload.cgi
```

In addition to the directives mentioned in the previous section, Apache provides directives that simplify associating specific MIME types, file extensions, or even specific HTTP methods with a particular CGI. The mod_actions module, included in the base distribution and compiled by default, provides the Action and Script directives, shown in this example:

- The Action directive accepts two arguments. The first argument is a handler or a MIME content type; the second points to the CGI program to handle the request.

- The Script directive associates certain HTTP request methods with a CGI program.

The information about the original requested document is passed to the CGI via the PATH_INFO (document URL) and PATH_TRANSLATED (document path) environment variables.

As with the example from the previous section, the directory containing the destination CGI must be marked as allowing CGI execution with either a ScriptAlias directive or the ExecCGI parameter to the Options directive.

Troubleshooting the Execution of CGI Scripts

```
ScriptLog logs/cgi_log
```

In addition to the modules and techniques explained in Chapter 2 and Chapter 3, the mod_cgi module provides the ScriptLog directive to aid in the debugging of CGI scripts. If enabled, it will store information for each failed CGI execution, including HTTP headers, POST variables, and so on. This file can grow quickly, so you can limit its growth with the ScriptLogBuffer and ScriptLogLength directives.

Improving CGI Script Performance

One of the main drawbacks of CGI development is the performance impact associated with the requirement to start and stop programs per every request.

mod_perl and FastCGI provide two solutions for this problem. Both require careful examination of existing code because you can no longer assume in your CGIs that all resources will be automatically freed by the operating system after the request is served.

mod_perl is a module available for Apache 1.3 and 2.0 that embeds a Perl interpreter inside the Apache web server. In addition to a powerful API to Apache internals, mod_perl includes a CGI compatibility mode that provides an environment that allows existing Perl CGIs to run with little or no modification. Since the scripts are run inside a persistent, in-process interpreter, there is no startup penalty.

FastCGI is a standard that allows the same instance of a CGI program to answer several requests over time. You can read the specs and download modules for Apache 1.3 and 2.x from http://www.fastcgi.com. FastCGI has regained some popularity by its use by web development frameworks such as Ruby-on-Rails.

Understanding Server Side Includes

```
Document on disk
This document, <!--#echo var="DOCUMENT_NAME" -->,
was last modified <!--#echo var="LAST_MODIFIED" -->

Content received by the browser
This document, sample.shtml,
was last modified Sunday, 14-Sep-2005 12:03:20 PST
```

SSI is a simple, "old school" web technology and a predecessor to other HTML embedded languages such as PHP. SSI provides a simple and effective mechanism for adding simple pieces of dynamic content with very little overhead; for example, a common footer for each page that includes the date and time the page was served. As another example, the Apache 2.0 distribution uses SSI to provide a custom look and feel for error messages. It works by embedding special processing instructions inside web pages and evaluating them before the content is returned to the client. You can learn more about Apache SSI support at http://httpd.apache.org/docs/2.0/howto/ssi.html.

Configuring Server Side Includes

```
AddType text/html .shtml
AddHandler server-parsed .shtml
```

Server side includes functionality is provided by the mod_include module, distributed with Apache. The simplest way to configure it is to associate an extension with the server-parsed content handler, as shown in the example.

Setting Environment Variables

```
SetEnv foo bar
UnSetEnv foo
PassEnv foo
```

Environment variables are variables that can be shared between modules and that are also available to external processes such as CGIs and server side include (SSI) documents. Environment variables also can be used for intermodule communication and to flag certain requests for special processing.

You can set environment variables with the SetEnv directive. This variable will be available to CGI scripts and SSI pages, and can be logged or added to a header. For example

```
SetEnv foo bar
```

will create the environment variable foo and assign it the value bar.

Conversely, you can remove specific variables using the UnsetEnv directive.

Finally, the PassEnv directive enables you to expose variables from the server process environment. For example

```
PassEnv LD_LIBRARY_PATH
```

will make the environment variable LD_LIBRARY_PATH available to CGI scripts and SSI pages. This variable contains the path to loadable dynamic libraries in some Unix systems, such as Linux. You can get a listing of standard environment variables in the appendix.

Accessing an Environment Variable

You can access an environment variable named foo from an SSI page with

```
<!--#echo var="foo" -->
```

You can log its value with the %{foo}e formatting option, as explained in Chapter 3, or you can add it to an HTTP header, as explained in Chapter 10 with

```
RequestHeader set X-Foo "%{foo}e"
```

Setting Environment Variables Dynamically

```
SetEnvIf HTTP_USER_AGENT MSIE iexplorer
SetEnvIf HTTP_USER_AGENT MSIE iexplorer=foo
SetEnvIf HTTP_USER_AGENT MSIE !javascript
```

The SetEnvIf directive enables you to set environment variables based on request information, such as the username, the file being requested, or a specific HTTP header value.

This directive takes a request parameter, a regular expression, and a set of variables that will be modified if the parameter matches the expression. This example matches Microsoft Internet Explorer browsers and shows how you can just set a variable, assign it an arbitrary value foo, or even assign it a negated expression.

Later, you can check the existence and value of this variable to perform a variety of actions such as logging a specific request or serving different content based on the type of browser. For example, you could provide simplified HTML pages for text browsers such as Lynx, or for PDA and cell phone browsers.

In fact, checking for the client user agent is so common that mod_setenvif provides the BrowserMatch directive, allowing you to simply write

```
BrowserMatch MSIE iexplorer=1
```

NOTE: Both SetEnvIf and BrowserMatch have non-case sensitive versions, SetEnvIfNoCase and BrowserMatchNoCase, that can be used to simplify the regular expressions in certain situations.

Special Environment Variables

```
BrowserMatch "Mozilla/2" nokeepalive
```

Apache provides a set of special environment variables. If one of those variables is set, Apache will modify its behavior. They are commonly used to work around buggy clients. For example, the `nokeepalive` variable disables keepalive support in Apache. This reduces performance on the server, since multiple requests cannot be transmitted over the same connection. Hence, it should only be set when the request is made by a client that does not correctly support this functionality, typically using a `BrowserMatch` or `SetEnvIf` directive, as shown in the example.

In the appendix you can find a list of all the special environment variables. Chapters 7 and 8 include examples of special variables used to work around issues with SSL and DAV implementations.

Understanding Content Negotiation

```
AddCharset UTF-8 .utf8
AddLanguage en .en
AddEncoding gzip .gzip .gz
```

The HTTP protocol provides mechanisms that enable you to maintain different versions of a certain resource and return the appropriate content based on the capabilities and preferences of the client. For example, a client may inform you that he is able to accept content that is compressed and that, while its preferred language is English, it will also understand pages written in Spanish. The three main aspects that are negotiated are

- Encoding: This is the format in which a resource is stored or represented, and can usually be determined from the file extension. For example, the file listing.txt.gz has a MIME type of text/plain and a gzip encoding. The encoding of the resource will be appended to the Content-Encoding: header of the response.

- Character Set: This property describes the particular character set used by a document. The character set of the resource will be appended to the Content-Type: header of the response, together with the MIME type.

- Language: You can provide different versions of the same resource. For example, the Apache documentation provides index.html.en, index.html.es, index.html.de, and so on. The language of the resource will be appended to the Content-Language: header of the response.

The example explains how you can associate charsets, languages, and encodings with particular file extensions.

Configuring Content Negotiation

```
Options +Multiviews
AddHandler type-map .var
```

There are two primary ways of configuring content negotiation in Apache: multiviews and type maps.

Multiviews can be enabled by adding an `Options` `+Multiviews` directive to your configuration. This method is not recommended (except for simple websites) because it is not very efficient: For every request, it scans the directory containing the file, looking for similar documents with additional extensions. It will then construct a list of such files and use the extensions to determine content encoding and character set, and return the appropriate content.

It is recommended that you use type maps instead, because they save filesystem lookups. These are special files that map filenames and information (metadata) about them. You can configure a type map for a certain resource by creating a file with the same name and the `.var` extension, and adding an `AddHandler` directive, as shown in the sample configuration.

The file can contain several entries. Each entry starts with a `URI:` that is the name of the document, followed by several attributes such as `Content-Type:`, `Content-Language:`, and `Content-Encoding:`. The following listing shows a sample type map file.

Listing 4.1   **Contents of Type Map File**

```
URI: page.html.en
Content-type: text/html
Content-language: en

URI: page.html.fr
Content-type: text/html; charset=iso-8859-2
Content-language: fr
```

TIP: Bear in mind that using any kind of content-negotiation has an adverse impact on the performance of the web server, as it requires additional filesystem accesses.

Assigning Default Charsets and Language Priorities

```
DefaultLanguage en
AddDefaultCharset iso-8859-1
LanguagePriority en es de
```

You can specify a default character set for documents without one already associated by using the AddDefaultCharset, as shown in the example. Another option is to specify AddDefaultcharset Off to disable adding a character set for documents without one associated.

You can specify a default language with the DefaultLanguage directive. For a website in English, that would be en, as shown in the example.

Finally, if the client does not provide a language preference, you can use LanguagePriority to determine the preferred language order. In this example, if a document in English is found, it will be served. Otherwise, Apache will look for a document in Spanish, and if that is not found, Apache will look for a document in German. You can learn more about this topic at http://httpd.apache.org/docs/2.0/mod/mod_negotiation.html and http://httpd.apache.org/docs/2.0/mod/mod_mime.html.

Advanced URL Mapping with mod_rewrite

Apache provides a very powerful module, mod_rewrite, that allows virtually unlimited URL manipulation capabilities using regular expressions. Due to its complexity, it is outside the scope of this book other than specific references or examples in other chapters. It is mentioned here so you are aware of its existence if you reach the limits of what Redirect, ErrorDocument, and Alias directives can do.

You can learn more about mod_rewrite at http://httpd.apache.org/docs/2.0/mod/mod_rewrite.html.

Understanding the "Trailing Slash" Problem

```
DirectorySlash On
```

Sometimes, certain URLs only work only if they have a "/" at the end. This is likely because you have either not loaded mod_dir into the server or because the redirections made by mod_dir are not working correctly with the value specified in the ServerName directive, as explained in the "Redirections Do Not Work" section in Chapter 2.

When accessing certain URLs that map into directories, it is necessary to add a trailing slash ("/") to the end of the URL to correctly access the content of the directory, which can be either an index file or a directory index. Forgetting to add this trailing slash is a common mistake, so when mod_dir realizes that may be happening, it issues the appropriate redirection.

For example, if mod_dir is enabled on the server, and you have a directory named foo under the document root, a request for http://example.com/foo will be redirected to http://example.com/foo/.

This is the default behavior in both Apache 1.3 and 2.0 when mod_dir is loaded into the server. In Apache 2, you can disable such redirections using a DirectorySlash directive:

```
DirectorySlash Off
```

Fixing Spelling Mistakes

```
CheckSpelling on
```

mod_speling is a useful Apache module that recognizes misspelled URLs and redirects the user to the correct location for the document. mod_speling is able to correct URLs with the wrong capitalization or with one letter missing or incorrect. This is most common when users misspell the URL while typing it in the browser.

For example, if a user requests the file file.html and it is not present, mod_speling will search for a similar document such as FILE.HTML, file.htm, and so on, and if it finds one, will return it. This has a performance impact, but can be quite useful and avoid unnecessary support requests due to broken links.

To enable spelling checks, you can add CheckSpelling on to your Apache configuration, as shown in the example.

NOTE: If there are several documents that may be a match for the misspelling, the module will return a list of those documents. This could have security implications because you may not want to make some of those files visible.

Fixing Capitalization Problems

```
NoCase on
```

Windows has a non–case sensitive file system, while Unix systems are case sensitive. This usually creates problems when migrating websites from Windows to Unix servers. All of a sudden, URLs such as http://www.example.com/images/icon.PNG that used to work fine on Windows start failing with Document Not Found errors, because the file on disk is named icon.png and is not equivalent on Unix to the icon.PNG file requested. This issue can be solved by manually checking and rewriting every link or by enabling the mod_speling module as described in the previous section.

There is also an alternative, single-purpose module that can be used to this end: mod_nocase. This module, originally based on mod_speling, makes GET request for URLs non–case sensitive. It checks for an exact URL match and if it does not find it, it tries a non–case sensitive matching. If multiple files match the non–case sensitive search, the first one will automatically be selected. To enable mod_nocase, you should load it into the server and include a NoCase directive in your Apache configuration file, as shown in the example.

You can download mod_nocase from http://www.misterblue.com/Software/mod_nocase.htm.

Remember that enabling either `mod_speling` or `mod_nocase` has an impact on the performance of the server.

Validating Your Pages with Tidy

```
AddOutputFilterByType    TIDY    text/html applica-
tion/xhtml+xml
TidyOption char-encoding utf8
```

Independently of whether you have dynamically gen-erated or hand-coded your HTML pages, if they con-tain markup errors, they may not display correctly in all browsers. Tidy is a useful command-line tool that is able to process malformed HTML and XML, correct many common mistakes, and produce standards-com-pliant output. You can download it from http://tidy.sourceforge.net/.

You can run Tidy from the command line over static files or, thanks to `mod_tidy` and the Apache 2 filter architecture, process content being served on-the-fly. This example shows how to use the `SetFilter` direc-tive to associate a Tidy filter with XML and HTML files and how to use `TidyOption` to configure the behavior of the Tidy engine. Apache filter architecture and configuration is described in Chapter 11. You can download `mod_tidy` from

`http://home.snafu.de/tusk/mod_tidy/.`

A related Apache 2 module is `mod_validator`, which can be downloaded from

`http://www.webthing.com/software/mod_validator/.`

Virtual Hosting

This chapter explains how to host multiple websites with a single instance of the Apache server, using both IP-address–based and name-based virtual hosting. It also covers other topics related to providing hosting for multiple users, such as home directories and per-directory configuration files.

What Is Virtual Hosting?

Virtual hosting is a feature provided by most modern web servers that allows you to serve multiple websites, each one identified by one or more domains, using a single instance of a server. This provides for a centralized administration and an efficient use of system resources. Many commercial web hosting providers are able to provide service to hundreds of customers using a single server instance instead of having hundreds of Apache servers running in the background.

What Is IP-based Virtual Hosting?

```
<VirtualHost 192.168.200.4:80>
(...)
</VirtualHost>
```

The easiest way to provide virtual hosting is based on the IP address/port combination that the client connects to. We can configure Apache to support IP-based virtual hosting using `<VirtualHost>` sections. Each `<VirtualHost>` contains configuration directives that will be applied for requests addressed to the IP address (and optionally port number) specified in the opening tag. Of course, the server Apache is running on must have been configured with those IP addresses.

NOTE: If you are listening on nonstandard ports, make sure to provide a `Listen` directive for each one of them. Just listing them on the `<VirtualHost>` section will not cause Apache to listen for request in those ports.

IP-based virtual hosting has the drawback of having to assign a different IP address to each different virtual host.

Configuring IP-based Virtual Hosting

The example in Listing 5.1 shows three IP-based virtual hosts serving content for three websites: www.example.com, a staging version of www.example.com, and www.example.net. The `ServerName` directive inside each container will be used for

constructing self-referential URLs. The DocumentRoot
directive specifies a different location for the website's
content for each virtual host. It is also possible to log
requests and errors for each virtual host to a different
file. This can be done by placing logging directives
such as TransferLog and ErrorLog inside the virtual
host container, as explained in Chapter 3.

The addresses and ports listed inside the opening tag
of a <VirtualHost> definition will not have any effect
on what addresses or ports Apache listens to, so you
still need to provide the appropriate Listen directives.
If no port is specified in a <VirtualHost> definition, the
one specified in the most recent Apache directive will
be used. It is also possible to specify a wildcard "*" to
listen for requests in all ports that Apache is listening
in, as shown in the example.net virtual host.

Listing 5.1   Configuring IP-Based Virtual Hosts

```
Listen 8080
Listen 80
<VirtualHost 192.168.200.2>
    ServerName www.example.com
    DocumentRoot /usr/local/apache/sites/example.com
</VirtualHost>

<VirtualHost 192.168.200.2:8080>
    ServerName www.example.com
    DocumentRoot /usr/local/apache/sites/staging
</VirtualHost>

<VirtualHost 192.168.200.4:*>
    ServerName www.example.net
    DocumentRoot /usr/local/apache/sites/example.net
</VirtualHost>
```

What Is Name-based Virtual Hosting?

As seen in the previous sections, IP virtual hosting requires a different IP address for each website. This creates quite a few problems if you need to host a great number of websites or you cannot get or do not want to pay for more than one IP address. An example where this would be the case would be if you wanted to run several personal websites out of your own server at the end of a DSL line.

Name-based virtual hosting takes advantage of the fact that most browsers in widespread use (and almost all recent ones) transmit a `Host:` header in their HTTP request. This is a requirement of the HTTP/1.1 protocol, but is also present in most implementations of HTTP/1.0. Thus, we can decide which information to present to the user based on data from the HTTP request, rather than on data from the connection itself. This allows several virtual hosts to share the same IP address and port combination.

Configuring Name-based Virtual Hosting

The configuration for named virtual hosts is similar to IP virtual hosts. The example in Listing 5.2 shows two virtual hosts sharing the 192.168.200.2 IP address.

Apache will decide to which virtual host to "route" the request based on the value of the `Host:` header of the HTTP request. It will be compared for a match with the hostname provided by `ServerName` and any additional hostnames provided by the `ServerAlias` directives, which are optional.

Listing 5.2   Configuring Name-based Virtual Hosts

```
Listen 80
NameVirtualHost 192.168.200.2
<VirtualHost 192.168.200.2>
    ServerName www.example.com
    ServerAlias example.com web.example.com
    DocumentRoot /usr/local/apache/sites/example.com
</VirtualHost>

<VirtualHost 192.168.200.2>
    ServerName www.example.net
    DocumentRoot /usr/local/apache/sites/example.net
</VirtualHost>
```

The `NameVirtualHost` directive is required to tell Apache that a particular IP address will be used for name-based virtual hosts. You can tell Apache to use any available IP address for name-based virtual hosting with

```
NameVirtualHost *
```

Of course, your DNS servers need to be configured properly so the domains www.example.com, example.com, and web.example.com resolve to the 192.168.200.2 address.

What Happens If a Request Does Not Match Any Virtual Host?

If a request does not match any virtual host then it will be served by the main server in the case of IP-based virtual hosting. In the case of name-based virtual hosting, the first name-based virtual host will be used. See the next couple of sections for details on how to configure a default catch-all virtual host.

Configuring a Default Name-based Virtual Host

```
NameVirtualHost *
<VirtualHost *>
...
</VirtualHost>
```

As mentioned in the previous section, the first virtual host present in the configuration file will answer requests for domains that are not explicitly handled by other virtual hosts. If you host multiple websites, it can be useful to set up that virtual host so it returns a page that either provides a list of available websites in the machine or explains why that particular website is not recognized. You can do so by placing such a file (default.html in the example in Listing 5.3) in the document root and redirecting all requests to it with an AliasMatch directive. You can achieve a similar effect replacing it with an ErrorDocument directive:

```
ErrorDocument 404 /default.html
```

Or you can even send users directly to one of your other websites with a Redirect directive.

```
RedirectMatch /* http://www.example.com
```

Listing 5.3 **Configuring a Default Name-based Virtual Host**

```
NameVirtualHost *
# The section below needs to be placed on top of any
other virtual host section
<VirtualHost *>
ServerName default.example.com
DocumentRoot /usr/local/apache/sites/default
AliasMatch /* /default.html
</VirtualHost>
```

Configuring a Default IP-based Virtual Host

```
<VirtualHost _default_ >
ServerName default.example.com
DocumentRoot /usr/local/apache/sites/default
</VirtualHost>
```

The special _default_ syntax allows you to define a virtual host that will serve requests for addresses and port combinations not covered by other virtual hosts. You can also specify a port number in combination with the _default_ keyword, as in the following example, taken from the default Apache mod_ssl configuration. It specifies a virtual host that will listen for requests on that particular port, in all addresses not explicitly handled by other virtual hosts:

```
<VirtualHost _default_:443>
SSLEngine on
ServerName secure.example.com:443
DocumentRoot /usr/local/apache/sites/default
...
</VirtualHost>
```

Mixing Name-based and IP-based Virtual Hosts

It is possible to mix and match IP-based and name-based virtual hosts, as shown in Listing 5.4. Instead of using NameVirtualHost *, you will need to provide separate NameVirtualHost directives for each IP address that will be associated with name-based virtual hosts. This example shows two name-based virtual hosts associated with the 192.168.200.2 IP address and one IP-based virtual host associated with IP address 192.168.200.4.

Listing 5.4   Mixing IP-based and Name-based Virtual Hosting

```
NameVirtualHost 192.168.200.2
<VirtualHost 192.168.200.2>
    ServerName www.example.com
    DocumentRoot /usr/local/apache/sites/example.com
</VirtualHost>

<VirtualHost 192.168.200.2>
    ServerName staging.example.com
    DocumentRoot /usr/local/apache/sites/staging
</VirtualHost>
```

Listing 5.4   **Continued**

```
<VirtualHost 192.168.200.4>
    ServerName www.example.net
    DocumentRoot /usr/local/apache/sites/example.net
</VirtualHost>
```

Debugging Virtual Host Setups

You can invoke the httpd binary with the -S option, as shown in Listing 5.5, and Apache will parse the configuration file. After processing all of the virtual host related information, it will present you with information about each configured virtual host and default host values. This is a very handy tool for debugging complex virtual host setups.

Listing 5.5   Checking the Virtual Host Configuration

```
# httpd -S
VirtualHost configuration:
wildcard NameVirtualHosts and _default_ servers:
*:*                     is a NameVirtualHost
        default server example.com
(/usr/local/www/conf/httpd.conf:1055)
        port * namevhost example.com
(/usr/local/www/conf/httpd.conf:1055)
        port * namevhost example.org
(/usr/local/www/conf/httpd.conf:1082)
        port * namevhost example.net
(/usr/local/www/conf/httpd.conf:1094)
Syntax Ok
```

Using SSL with Name-based Virtual Hosts

The short answer is that SSL cannot be used with name-based virtual hosts, as there are currently no mainstream browsers that support it. See the related section in Chapter 7 for a more in-depth explanation.

Alternate Virtual Hosting

```
UseCanonicalName Off
VirtualDocumentRoot /usr/local/apache/vhosts/%0
VirtualScriptAlias \
    /usr/local/apache/vhosts/%0/cgi-bin
```

If you maintain a great number of virtual hosts, it may be desirable to use a different approach for virtual hosting. This is particularly true for ISPs that host thousands of customers, as it would require entering details for each one of the virtual hosts in the configuration file and restarting the server each time a change is required.

The mod_virtualhost_alias allows you to set up a different document root for each virtual host dynamically. This means that the request is mapped to a certain path on the file system based on information from the request itself, such as the IP address or the hostname. This example maps requests for a particular hostname to a path in the file system that includes that hostname (represented by the %0 in the path). Similarly, the VirtualScriptAlias directive allows execution of CGI scripts in a directory path based on the hostname referred to by the request. If a user sends a request for /manual/index.html to the www.example.com host, this

directive will map that to /usr/local/apache/vhosts/
www.example.com/manual/index.html.

In a similar manner , you can map IP addresses instead
of hostnames, for IP-based virtual hosting using the
VirtualDocumentRootIP and VirtualScriptAliasIP directives.

You can decide to map requests based only on parts of
the hostname or IP address or based on the port of the
request. For that, you can use different %-based
sequences, such as %p for the port number, or %1 for
the first part of the domain, %2 for the second, and
so on.

Alternate Virtual Hosting Modules

The mod_vhost_alias module is probably one of the
most popular mass virtual host modules, due to the
fact that is bundled with Apache. There are, however, a
number of alternatives such as the following:

- mod_vhost_ldap: An Apache 2 module that allows
  you to store virtual host information inside an
  LDAP directory. It can be downloaded from
  http://alioth.debian.org/projects/modvhostldap/.

- mod_vhost_dbi: This module allows you to store
  virtual host configuration inside a SQL database
  and provides a great amount of flexibility. It runs
  on Apache 2 and can be obtained from http://
  www.outoforder.cc/projects/apache/
  mod_vhost_dbi/.

Chapter 11 covers a number of Multi-Processing Modules (MPMs), such as mod_perchild, that allow you to run different virtual hosts under different user ids.

Per-directory Configuration Files

```
AccessFilename .htaccess
```

An issue related to hosting multiple websites is that of providing hosting services for multiple clients. If the number of clients is significant, you may want to use per-directory configuration files. Per-directory config- uration files are usually called htaccess files because they used to be used mostly for access control tasks. When this functionality is enabled, Apache will look for special configuration files in all directories leading to the file being requested. For example, if Apache receives a request for /usr/local/apache2/htdocs/index.html, it will look for per-directory configuration files in the /, /usr/, /usr/local/, /usr/local/apache2, and /usr/local/apache2/htdocs directories, in that order.

If found, the content for these configuration files is processed and merged with the main configuration from httpd.conf read at startup time. This is quite con- venient for the system administrator, as it can allow users to self-manage their configurations. Also, since the files are parsed on-the-fly, the server does not need to be restarted for each change. On the downside, this has a performance penalty. Apache must perform expensive disk operations looking for these files in every request, even if the files do not exist.

The directive `AccessFilename` allows you to provide a list of filenames that Apache will look for when looking for per-directory configuration files.

Controlling the Scope of Per-directory Configuration Files

`AllowOverride Indexes Limit AuthConfig`

If `.htaccess` is present in the `Context:` field in the directive reference syntax description of the Apache documentation, it means that directive can be placed in per-directory configuration files.

The `AllowOverride` directive allows you to control the kind of configuration directives that can appear in per-directory configuration files. For example, you can let users change directory-indexing directives but not those related to authorization. Possible values are

- `Authconfig`: Authorization directives
- `FileInfo`: Directives controlling document types
- `Indexes`: Directives controlling directory indexing
- `Limit`: Host access control directives
- `Options`: Directives controlling specific directory features
- `All`: All directives belonging to above groups can be used
- `None`: Disable per-directory configuration files for that directory tree

Disabling Per-directory Configuration Files

```
<Directory />
AllowOverride None
</Directory>
```

If you do not have a use for per-directory configuration files, you can disable this functionality altogether with the configuration shown here. This will increase the security and performance of the server, at the cost of the flexibility and convenience provided by these files.

Security and Access Control

Understanding the Need for Access Control

Access control is a requirement for many websites. This means that certain content or areas of the website are only accessible to clients that come from a particular range of IP addresses or provide a valid username and password, for example. Access control can be implemented at a variety of levels, including at the operating-system level with packet filtering rules and at the web application level with forms, sessions, and cookies. This chapter deals exclusively with implementing access control, authentication, and authorization using the bundled Apache modules. This chapter also explains how different configuration settings can affect the security of your server and details a number of steps that you can take to improve it.

Apache provides a number of modules that allow you to control access to your content. The two main ones are mod_access, which allows controlling access based on the origin IP address and other characteristics of the request, and mod_auth, which authenticates users based on a username and password.

There are a number of other modules that will be mentioned in this chapter but will not be covered in detail because they are not used as often.

Differences Between Apache Versions

Apache's authorization and authentication framework was completely overhauled in Apache 2.2. Although most of the changes have occurred at the source code level, there are a number of user-visible changes. For the sake of clarity and because most of the basic concepts still apply, this chapter will primarily describe Apache 1.3 and 2.0 configuration. The Apache 2.2-specific changes will be discussed in the "Apache 2.2" section, later in the chapter.

Understanding Basic and Digest Authentication

You authenticate users of your website for tracking or authorization purposes. The HTTP specification provides two authentication mechanisms: basic and digest. In both cases, the process is the following:

1. A client tries to access restricted content in the web server.

2. Apache checks whether the client is providing a username and password. If not, Apache returns an

HTTP 401 status code, indicating that user authentication is required.

3. The client reads the response and prompts the user for the required username and password (usually with a pop-up window).

4. The client retries accessing the web page, this time transmitting the username and password as part of the HTTP request. The client remembers the username and password and transmits them in later requests to the same site, so the user does not need to retype them for every request.

5. Apache checks the validity of the credentials and grants or denies access based on the user identity and other access rules.

In basic authentication, the username and password are transmitted in clear text, as part of the HTTP request headers. This poses a security risk because an attacker could easily peek at the conversation between server and browser, learn the username and password, and reuse them freely afterward. Digest authentication provides increased security because it transmits a digest instead of the clear-text password. A digest algorithm is a mathematical operation that takes a text and returns another text, a digest, which uniquely identifies the original one. If a text changes, so does the digest. The digest is based on a combination of several parameters, including the username, password, and request method. The server can calculate the digest on its own and check that the client knows the password, even when the password itself is not transmitted over the network.

Unfortunately, although the specification has been available for quite some time, not all browsers support digest authentication or do it in a compatible manner.

In any case, for both digest and basic authentication, the requested information itself is transmitted unprotected over the network. A better choice to secure access to your website involves using SSL, as explained in Chapter 7.

Introducing Apache Access Control

```
<Directory /usr/local/apache2/htdocs/private>
    Order Allow, Deny
    Allow from 192.168.0 example.com
    Deny from guest-terminal.example.com
</Directory>
```

The example shows a sample configuration using IP and hostname-based access control with mod_access. Allow directives specify which individual IP addresses, networks, and hostnames have access to the content. Deny directives specify which ones will be denied. The Order directive specifies how Allow and Deny directives are evaluated.

In this example, the Order Allow,Deny directive specifies that Allow directives are to be evaluated first and Deny directives will be evaluated last. The order in which the directives are evaluated is important, and in this case the Deny directive will take precedence. Also, Order Allow,Deny ensures that if the client does not match any Allow directive, it will be denied access by default. Don't worry if you are a bit confused about how access control works. It is really easy once you understand the way directives are evaluated.

Introducing Apache Authorization and Authentication Configuration

```
<Directory /usr/local/apache2/htdocs/private>
AuthType Basic
AuthName "Password Protected Area"
AuthUserFile /usr/local/apache2/conf/htusers
Require user admin
</Directory>
```

The listing shows a sample configuration snippet that password-protects a directory. AuthType defines the authentication type: in this case, HTTP basic authentication. AuthName associates a text with the area that will be password-protected. This text will be presented to the user when the browser prompts her for a password (usually in a separate pop-up window). The AuthUserFile points to the user database and the Require directive specifies a user who will be granted access upon successful authentication. The following sections include more details on the previous example as well as instructions on how to create and manipulate the user database and how to combine IP and user-based control access, as shown in the "Combining Access Control Methods" section.

Creating a User Database

```
htpasswd  -c file userid
```

To create a user database (also known as a *password file*), you can use the htpasswd utility included with Apache. The syntax to create a new password file and add a user to it on Unix is shown in the example. On Windows, you will need to use

```
htpasswd.exe -cm file userid
```

If you want to add a new user to an existing password file, the syntax on Unix is simply

```
htpasswd  file userid
```

and on Windows

```
htpasswd.exe -m file userid
```

You will be asked for a password and it will be added to the user database.

You should not keep the password file in any directory accessible from the Web. You should not use -c when adding users to an existing file, as this will destroy the previous contents.

As an example, the following line creates a password file named htusers and adds a user named admin:

```
htpasswd  -c /usr/local/apache2/conf/htusers admin
```

Using Require to Authorize Users and Groups

```
<Directory /usr/local/apache2/htdocs/private>
    AuthType Basic
    AuthName "Password Protected Area"
    AuthUserFile /usr/local/apache2/conf/htusers
    AuthGroupFile /usr/local/apache2/conf/groups
    Require group administrators
</Directory>
```

You can instruct Apache to allow access to any valid user in the database that successfully authenticates with

```
Require valid-user
```

If you need to authorize only a certain group of users, you can explicitly list them in the arguments to Require:

```
Require user userid1 userid2
```

If you have a great number of users, a more convenient way to accomplish this is to use the AuthGroupFile directive. This directive points to a file containing group information in the following format:

```
groupname: userid1 userid2 userid3 [..]
```

For example

```
administrators: admin boss
users: admin boss user1 user2
```

The example at the beginning of this section shows a configuration snippet that allows access only to those users that successfully authenticate themselves and also belong to the group administrators. In this example, that would mean users admin and boss.

Handling a Large Number of Users

```
<DirectoryMatch /home/*/public_html>
    AuthType Basic
    AuthName "Private Area"
    AuthDBMUserFile /usr/local/apache2/conf/dbmusers
    AuthDBMGroupFile /usr/local/apache2/conf/dbmusers
    AuthDBMAuthoritative on
    Require group student faculty
</DirectoryMatch>
```

The mod_auth_dbm module is equivalent in functionality to mod_auth, but stores user data in a file-based database, speeding data lookup when there is a large number of users. This module provides a number of directives such as AuthDBMAuthoritative, AuthDBMUserFile, and AuthDBMGroupFile, which are equivalent in syntax and functionality to the plain-text ones provided by mod_auth. To manipulate the user and group files, you will need to use htdbm and dbmmanage, the counterparts to mod_auth's tools. Note that group and user data can be stored in the same database, as shown here.

Allowing Access Only to Specific IP Addresses

```
<Directory /usr/local/apache2/htdocs/private>
    Order Allow, Deny
    Allow from 192.168.0
</Directory>
```

Sometimes, it is desirable to restrict access to certain content (such as a company's internal website) to specific IP addresses, such as those coming from an internal network. This example will allow access to the directory /usr/local/apache2/htdocs/private and its subdirectories only to clients with IP addresses in the range 192.168.0.1 to 192.168.0.254.

The argument passed to the Directory container must literally match the filesystem path that Apache uses to access the files.

The line Order Allow, Deny denies access by default and only clients that match the Allow directive will be granted access. The Allow directive can accept multiple individual IP addresses or a certain address range of IP addresses. Check the directive reference for details.

You can also allow access only to specific IP addresses using the same code in a .htaccess file in /usr/local/apache2/htdocs/private:

```
Order Allow,Deny
Allow from 192.168.0
```

Denying Access to Specific IP Addresses

```
<Directory /usr/local/apache2/htdocs/private>
    Order Deny,Allow
    Deny from 192.168.0.2 192.168.0.5
</Directory>
```

Conversely to what was explained in the previous section, it is possible to allow general access but deny access when the request comes from a specific IP address or range of IP addresses. This is useful, for example, to block specific machines or web crawlers that have been a source of problems or bandwidth abuse.

This example will allow access to the directory /usr/local/apache2/htdocs/private and its subdirectories to anybody except clients with the IP addresses 192.168.0.2 and 192.168.0.5.

Allow and Deny can also restrict access based on the presence of an environment variable, as explained in the "Restricting Access Based on the Browser Type" section, later in this chapter.

Chapter 9 deals with additional ways of restricting or slowing down access to misbehaving clients.

Combining Access Control Methods

```
<Location /restricted>
 Allow from 192.168.200.0/255.255.255.0
 AuthType Basic
 AuthUserFile /usr/local/apache2/conf/htusers
 AuthName "Restricted Resource"
 AuthAuthoritative on
 Require valid-user
 Satisfy any
</Location>
```

You can combine different access control methods using the Satisfy directive. For example, the configuration shown here requires users to either come from an internal, authorized address OR provide a valid username and password.

If you would like to require both that user come from a certain internal address AND provide a valid username and password, you will need to use Satisfy all.

Customizing Your Access Denied Page

When a request gets an access denied response from the web server, the user will be presented with a hard-coded server-generated error message. You can customize the message the user receives using the ErrorDocument directive in three different ways:

You can show the user a custom message, as in the following example

```
ErrorDocument 403 "You do not have permission to
access this file"
```

if you are using Apache 2 or

```
ErrorDocument 403 "You do not have permission to
access this file
```

if you are using Apache 1.3 (notice that there is only
one double-quote, at the beginning of the string).

Alternatively, you can redirect the request to a local
URL-path with a custom message:

```
ErrorDocument 401 /login_failed.html
```

In this case, the file passed to the directive as the second argument is a path starting with a slash (/), relative
to the value specified in the directive `DocumentRoot`.

Finally, you can redirect the request to an external
URL:

```
ErrorDocument 404 http://www.example.com/page
_not_found.html
```

These examples referred to different 400 HTTP return
codes, which indicate there was an error resolving the
request, such as the user not providing a correct username and password. You can of course do the same for
other common HTTP codes such as internal server
errors. You can find a complete listing of HTTP return
codes in the appendix.

NOTE: Some versions of Microsoft Internet Explorer (MSIE)
will by default ignore server-generated error messages
when they are less than 512 bytes in size, so be sure to
specify a message greater than that. You can learn more
about this issue in this Microsoft Knowledge Base article
http://support.microsoft.com/default.aspx?scid=
kb;en-us;Q294807.

Putting Users in Control

If you have multiple users publishing content in your Apache installation, it is very convenient to allow them to password-protect their own directories using .htaccess files, described in Chapter 1. This mechanism has a performance penalty but relieves you of the task of providing access to or updating the Apache configuration file or user databases each time a change is required.

In the appropriate directory sections of your Apache configuration file, you will need to add

```
AllowOverride AuthConfig Limit
```

This will enable your users to create their own .htaccess configuration files and place their own access control and authorization-related directives there.

Conversely, you can prevent per-directory configuration changes with the following global setting:

```
<Directory />
AllowOverride none
</Directory>
```

This has the added bonus of improving performance, since Apache does not need to look for the existence of per-directory configuration files for each file requested. Alternatively, you could restrict the type of configuration options that are allowed. For more information, check the documentation for AllowOverride.

Denying Access to System and Sensitive Files

```
<Files ~ "^\.ht">
 Order allow,deny
 Deny from all
</Files>
```

There are certain types of files that we do not want our visitors to access under any circumstances, because they may contain passwords or other sensitive information. These include example backup files created by Unix text editors, per-directory configuration files, and so on. You may want to deny access to them using explicit configuration settings such as those shown here, which are included by default in the Apache configuration and deny access to .htaccess and .htpasswd files.

It is also possible to prevent the server from delivering unintended content by configuring it not to follow symbolic links. For this purpose, use the FollowSymLinks and SymLinksIfOwnerMatch arguments to the Options directive, as described in its documentation.

You may also want to disable mod_speling, explained in Chapter 4 as sometimes it may accidentally expose the names of files not intended for publishing when a misspelled URL could match multiple documents.

See also the section on how to restrict access to directory listings.

Restricting Program Execution

CGI programs can be a security risk. It is advisable that you disable CGI execution or at least restrict it to specific directories. For that purpose, do not use AddHandler directives to globally enable CGI execution of certain file extensions.

Similarly, mod_include allows execution of CGIs and external commands using Server Side Includes. They are disabled by default by the Options -IncludesNoExec directive. If possible, make sure that the directories containing CGI scripts are writable only by the superuser and not by anyone else, and especially not by the user Apache is running as.

On a related note, you should make sure that, whenever possible, the document tree is read only. This will prevent an attacker from creating a file that can later be executed. An example of this would be to introduce a file containing PHP code in a PHP-enabled server. Also, make sure to password-protect DAV-enabled directories and do not make website contents available through other services such as FTP.

Preventing Abuse

There are a number of ways in which you can restrict or slow down access to all or part of your website. This is useful when you do not want certain content to be available in search engines or when a misbehaving web crawler consumes too many resources. These methods are explained in detail in Chapter 9 which also covers how to avoid or minimize denial-of-service attacks. Denial-of-service attacks are designed to prevent or severely impair the ability of your server to answer your users' requests. A number of Apache modules and settings can help to reduce in part those issues.

Disabling Directory Listings

```
<Directory /usr/local/apache2/htdocs/private>
    Options -Indexes
</Directory>
```

Apache allows you to define special index files with the DirectoryIndex directive. When a request is made by a client that maps into a directory path, Apache looks for one of those index files (usually named index.html or home.html) and returns it to the browser. Alternatively, if no such file is found, Apache will return an HTML page containing a listing of the directory. While this is useful during development, or when making available a file repository, it can also provide the names of files that you do not want published or indexed by search engines (such as backup files). You can disable directory listings by disabling the mod_autoindex module or using the Options directive as shown here.

If per-directory configuration files are enabled, you can also place the example in an .htaccess file.

Changing the Server: Header

```
ServerTokens Prod
```

Apache returns a Server: header with every request. By default, this header includes information about the server name, version, and platform. Other modules present in the server, such as SSL, PHP, or mod_perl, may add additional entries to the server string containing the module name and version. You can change or restrict the server header information using the `ServerTokens` directive. While it is always good to minimize the amount of information about the server configuration that is leaked to the external world, changing the server string will not bring much additional security: Most automated scan and attack tools will ignore this information and just probe for vulnerable scripts and modules one after another, regardless of the version and modules reported.

Preventing Hotlinking to Your Images

```
RewriteEngine On
RewriteCond %{HTTP_REFERER}
    !^http://(www\.)?example\.com/ [NC]
RewriteCond %{HTTP_REFERER} ^http:// [NC]
RewriteCond %{HTTP_REFERER} !^$
RewriteRule \.(jpg|jpeg|gif|png|bmp)$ - [F]
```

Sometimes, people will link directly from their website to resources on your server, such as logo images and binary program files. This is called *hotlinking* and in certain situations, you may want to prevent this from happening. For example, a certain online-merchant realized that half its traffic (and bandwidth bill) was from other sites hotlinking to its images for credit card companies and countries.

You can prevent people from hotlinking to your images by requiring that the requests to the images come from your server. You can do so using `mod_rewrite`. The example in the listing here will return a Forbidden answer to any request made for image files (identified by their extensions in the fourth RewriteCond line) whose HTTP_REFERER header does not match your domain name (first RewriteCond line). In addition, since certain browsers may not send a valid referer field or not send one at all, additional checks are performed to see that the referer field starts with http:// and is not blank (second and third RewriteCond lines).

Restricting Specific HTTP Methods

```
<Directory /home/*/public_html>
 AllowOverride FileInfo AuthConfig Limit
 Options MultiViews Indexes SymLinksIfOwnerMatch
     IncludesNoExec
 <Limit GET POST OPTIONS PROPFIND>
  Order allow,deny
  Allow from all
 </Limit>
 <LimitExcept GET POST OPTIONS PROPFIND>
   Order deny,allow
   Deny from all
 </LimitExcept>
</Directory>
```

You can control access to your server based on the HTTP method of the request using <Limit> and <LimitExcept> directives. This example, taken from the default Apache configuration file, shows how to allow read-only methods and deny requests for any other methods that can modify the content of the file system, such as PUT. The <Directory> section identifies per-user directories that can contain web pages, as explained in Chapter 8. The next two lines restrict the configuration settings that can be changed by users and other security settings. The <Limit> section allows access by default to those HTTP methods that are read-only, such as GET and POST. The <LimitExcept> section does the opposite, denying access to any other method, without explicitly having to enumerate them.

This is particularly useful in the context of allowing your users to administer their own content, as covered in Chapter 8.

Restricting Access Based on the Browser Type

```
SetEnvIf User-Agent ^EvilSearchEngine broken_crawler
<Directory /usr/local/apache2/htdocs>
    Order Deny,Allow
    Deny from env=broken_crawler
</Directory>
```

You can restrict access based on the browser type or any other header information or connection property by using environment variables with Allow and Deny.

In this case, browsers with a User-Agent header beginning with EvilSearchEngine will be denied access, and all others will be allowed. This is accomplished by using the SetEnvIf directive to conditionally set an environment variable named broken_crawler if the User-Agent header of the request (first argument) matches a certain regular expression (second argument). Later on, you can conditionally apply Deny and Allow directives based on the existence of that environment variable, identified by an env= prefix. Bear in mind that, although this technique will work most of the time, since the headers are sent by the client, headers cannot really be trusted.

Using Location and Directory Sections

The `Order` directive controls the order of access directive processing only within each phase of the server's configuration processing. This implies, for example, that an `Allow` or `Deny` directive occurring in a `<Location>` section will always be evaluated after an `Allow` or `Deny` directive occurring in a `<Directory>` section or `.htaccess` file, regardless of the setting of the `Order` directive.

Take into account that symbolic links and `Alias` directives may affect your authentication setup. For example, your restrictions may be bypassed if your access control directives are placed inside a `<Location>` container but the content is also accessible through additional URL mappings.

Additional Authentication Modules

In addition to the main modules that provide IP-based access control and the standard basic and digest authentication, Apache bundles a number of other authentication modules, such as

- `mod_auth_anon`: Provides for FTP-style "anonymous" user access to file-download areas.
- `mod_auth_ldap`: This module, available in Apache 2 and later, allows authenticating users against an LDAP directory.
- `mod_ssl`: This module is covered in detail in Chapter 7 and allows you to use certificate-based client authentication.

One of the virtues of Apache is that it is modular and extensible. A number of third-party modules have been developed that allow Apache to interface with existing authentication frameworks such as Windows domains, LDAP, PAM, and NIS, and user information stored in a variety of databases such as MySQL, PostgreSQL, Oracle, and others. You can find most of those modules at http://modules.apache.org and http://freshmeat.net.

You can always manage authentication at the application level. Usually, this is accomplished by requesting the username and password in a web form and, upon validation, assigning a cookie that authenticates the user for the rest of the session. This is how popular portal and ecommerce sites manage their personalization features.

mod_security

This module deserves a special mention. It is, in essence, an HTTP-level firewall. It allows you to inspect HTTP requests and perform all kind of monitoring, reporting, and access-control operations. It can detect and block common application-level attacks such as those involving SQL-injection and path transversal. You can find more information about this module at http://www.modsecurity.org.

Apache 2.2

```
<Location /combined>
    AuthType Basic
    AuthName "Restricted Access"
    AuthBasicProvider file ldap
    AuthUserFile /usr/local/apache2/conf/htusers
    AuthLDAPURL ldap://example.com/o=Sample
    Require valid-user
</Location>
```

Apache 2.2 includes significant changes to how authentication and authorization are implemented in Apache. The changes mostly relate to work that was performed in existing modules to clearly separate methods (basic and digest authentication) and providers (file, LDAP, or SQL backends, for example). Before, both functions were mixed in each module's implementation.

For example, `mod_authn_file` implements authentication against text files and `mod_authn_dbm` authenticates against database files. They can be combined with `mod_auth_basic` and `mod_auth_digest`, which in turn implement Basic and Digest HTTP authentication. Additional modules provide authorization functionality that authorizes users based on data stored in LDAP or SQL databases or files, as well as on file ownership or origin IP addresses.

Providers can be mixed and matched, as shown in the example at the beginning of this section. A new module, `mod_authn_alias`, allows you to define complex authentication setups that can be referred by name elsewhere in the configuration file. This allows you for example to authenticate the same resource against two different LDAP servers.

Keeping Up to Date with Apache Security

As with any other server software, you need to keep up to date with new Apache releases, making sure you are aware of security issues and the patches or workarounds to address them. These URLs will help you with this task.

- Apache announcements mailing list : http://httpd.apache.org/lists.html
- Apache Security issues: http://httpd.apache.org/security_report.hml
- Apache Week: http://www.apacheweek.com
- Apache Security Tips: http://httpd.apache.org/docs-2.0/misc/security_tips.html

Security Checklist

It is often said that security is a process, not a feature. To keep your Apache installation secure, you will need to keep up to date with Apache security advisories and monitor your error and access logs. Since Apache does not run isolated from its environment, you will need to do the same at the operating system and application level. In fact, most remotely exploitable problems with Apache are due to problems at the application level, such as vulnerable wiki, PHP libraries, and components.

Having said this, the following is a step-by-step list of measures you can take to secure a default Apache installation.

Disable Unneeded Modules

The first step is to disable all modules that you are not using. If you compiled Apache with loadable module support, you can comment out the directives that load specific modules. You may need to comment out other directives present in the configuration file that relate to the disabled module. Here is a short list of the most important modules that you should remove if you are not using them, roughly in order of importance:

- PHP, mod_python, mod_mono, mod_perl, and any other server side language modules. Of course, you should only disable PHP if you are not using Apache to run PHP-based applications.

- mod_include, which provides Server Side Includes support.

- mod_cgi, which provides support for invoking external programs.

- mod_ssl, used to provide SSL/TLS support for securing communications between the browser and Apache.

- mod_proxy, which, if incorrectly configured, can allow outsiders to use your server to relay requests.

- mod_deflate, an Apache 2 filter for compressing output on the fly.

- mod_suexec, used to execute external programs under user IDs different from the one Apache is running as.

- mod_userdir, which allows users in Unix systems to host their own pages.

- mod_rewrite, which allows arbitrary mapping and rewriting of incoming URLs.

Additionally, in Apache 1.3 you can explicitly disable specific compiled-in modules by using the ClearModuleList directive and then explicitly enable modules using the AddModule directive.

Remove Sample Scripts

Most web server-side software and development environments include sample applications and scripts for demonstration or testing purposes. While useful, these samples are usually not coded with security in mind, and can be vulnerable to several attacks, mostly related to the program not properly escaping user input. These flaws often result in an attacker being able to execute arbitrary system commands, revealing the contents of other files, or being able to modify the database.

Make sure you remove all sample scripts and demo accounts shipped with your application servers, as well as your development environment and other web-based software you may have installed.

Limit or Disable CGI Execution and SSI

If you do not require CGI-script support, you should disable mod_cgi. If you require CGI support, you should limit the ability to execute scripts to specific directories. For example, you should scan your configuration for ScriptAlias directives and Options directives with ExecCGI arguments and make sure they are properly configured. Make sure that directories marked as containing executable scripts are not writable by others. You may also consider using the suExec CGI wrapper, included with Apache.

The same rationale can be applied to Server Side Includes functionality, which is provided by mod_include and allows execution of external commands, unless disabled by Options -IncludesNoExec.

Check File Permissions

On Unix systems, Apache is usually started as root; does a certain number of operations, such as binding to the appropriate port; and then changes its user ID to the one specified with the User directive. Because there are certain operations performed as root, it is critical to make sure that the log and configuration files, as well as the directories containing them, are not writable by other users. Make sure directories being marked as containing executable scripts or that can contain PHP scripts are not world writable and are not accessible through FTP or WebDAV, for example.

Limit or Disable Proxy Functionality

As with CGIs, you need to disable or restrict proxy support in your Apache installation. Otherwise, an open proxy can be used to perform attacks targeted at other websites or even to relay mail spam. If you are running Apache as a reverse proxy, you can disable "regular" proxy (forward-proxy functionality) with

```
ProxyRequests off
```

Restrict Access to Your Server by Default

The server should be configured in such a way that by default it denies access to documents on the server unless access is explicitly enabled. The following configuration snippet, extracted from the Apache Documentation, does just that:

```
<Directory />
    Order Deny,Allow
    Deny from all
```

```
</Directory>
<Directory /usr/local/apache2/htdocs>
    Order Deny,Allow
    Allow from all
</Directory>
```

See also earlier sections on how to disable directory listings.

SSL/TLS

This chapter gives you a brief introduction to the concepts behind SSL and provides a step-by-step guide on how to install and configure the mod_ssl Apache module. You will learn how to solve common SSL-related issues as well as how to create, sign, and install your server keys and certificates.

What Is SSL?

The SSL/TLS family of protocols (Secure Sockets Layer/Transport Layer Security) is used to secure communications between two end-points, usually a server and a client. When a browser accesses a web server using the HTTP protocol, the data is transmitted in the open. A third party that is able to intercept that conversation at one point in the network will be able to access and even modify the data being transmitted. A number of applications, such as making electronic payments over the Web and accessing sensitive corporate data, require a level of security that is not available from the HTTP protocol.

The HTTPS protocol or Secure HTTP was developed to address those concerns. It improves the security of the HTTP protocol by providing

- Confidentiality: Encrypting the data so it cannot be read by others
- Integrity: Assuring the data was not modified in-transit
- Authentication: Verifying the identity of the server (or client)

HTTPS encapsulates HTTP over the SSL/TLS family of protocols (Secure Sockets Layer/Transport Layer Security), which the rest of the chapters simply refer to as "SSL." The default port for the HTTPS protocol is 443, and HTTPS URLs are prefixed with https://.

As you probably have experienced, most browsers provide visual feedback, usually in the form of a padlock next to the address bar, when connected to a site using the HTTPS protocol.

How Does SSL Work?

When the user types https://www.example.com, the browser recognizes the https:// prefix and knows that it must use the HTTPS protocol to connect to the server. When no port is specified, the default HTTPS port, 443, is used.

Once a connection is established, the client requests the server certificate. A certificate is an electronic piece of data that describes the identity of an end-point in the SSL communication, and is explained later in the chapter. The certificate is then tested for validity.

Depending on whether the validation process suc-
ceeds, the connection process will continue or the user
will be informed and asked for confirmation.
Optionally, the client can also provide a certificate, and
the server will follow a similar validation process.

Once the identity of the server (and of the client, if
necessary) has been established, the next step is to
agree on a common encryption key. For that purpose,
the public keys of each party are used in an algorithm
to securely agree on a symmetric key. Later in this
chapter, you will learn more about encryption keys
and how to generate them. The agreement process is
secure against eavesdroppers because when you
encrypt information with the server's public key, only
the server will be able to decrypt it.

The handshake phase has concluded and now the
client and server can proceed with the regular
exchange of information. At this point, most browsers
will provide the user with visual feedback that the
connection is secure, usually with a closed padlock.

Compiling OpenSSL

```
# gunzip < openssl*.tar.gz | tar xvf -
# cd openssl*
# ./config --prefix=/usr/local/ssl --
openssldir=/usr/local/ssl/openssl
# make
# make install
```

mod_ssl is the Apache module that implements
HTTPS. The OpenSSL project provides the base
cryptographic libraries used by mod_ssl, as well as
command-line utilities for creating and manipulating
server certificates.

You can download a Windows binary build from the binaries section of the OpenSSL website at http://www.openssl.org. Most modern Unix-like systems include OpenSSL by default, or you can install it using the system package management tools. If that is not the case, or you require a newer version than the one available in your system, you can download the OpenSSL source code and install it as shown at the beginning of this section. The rest of this chapter assumes that you installed OpenSSL in /usr/local/ssl.

The openssl command line tool is included as part of the OpenSSL distribution and will be placed in /usr/local/ssl/bin/.

Encryption Keys

Encryption is the process of converting an existing message, the plaintext, into a new, encrypted message that will be completely unintelligible to an eavesdropper. Decryption is the reverse process, which transforms the encrypted message into the original plaintext.

Usually encryption and decryption processes involve an additional piece of information: a key. If both sender and receiver share the same key, the process is referred to as *symmetric cryptography*. If sender and receiver have different, complementary keys, the process is called *asymmetric* or *public key cryptography*. In public key cryptography, there is a pair of keys: one public and the other private. The public key can be made freely available, whereas the owner keeps the private key secret. These two keys are complementary; a message encrypted with one of the keys can be decrypted only by the other key.

Creating a Key Pair

```
# ./usr/local/ssl/bin/openssl genrsa -rand
file1:file2:file3 \
   -out www.example.com.key 1024
625152 semi-random bytes loaded
Generating RSA private key, 1024 bit long modulus
.....++++++
.......................++++++
e is 65537 (0x10001)
```

The example shows how to create a key pair using the openssl command line tool.

genrsa indicates to OpenSSL that you want to generate a key pair using the RSA algorithm.

The rand switch is used to provide OpenSSL with random data to ensure that the generated keys are unique and unpredictable. Substitute file1, file2, and so on, for the path to several large, relatively random files for this purpose (such as a kernel image, compressed log files, and so on). This switch is not necessary on Windows because the random data is automatically generated by other means.

The out switch indicates where to store the results.

1024 indicates the number of bits of the generated key.

Creating a Password-protected Key Pair

```
# ./usr/local/ssl/bin/openssl genrsa -des3 -rand
file1:file2:file3 \
   -out www.example.com.key 1024
```

In this case, the des3 option indicates that the private key should be encrypted and protected by a pass phrase, and you will be asked to provide it. You will be asked for it whenever you want to start the server as shown in the SSLPassPhraseDialog section.

Remove the Password from a Key

```
# ./usr/local/ssl/bin/openssl rsa -in
www.example.com.key \
    -out www.example.com.key.unsecure
```

You can choose to unprotect the key by issuing this command. This has some security implications; please see the SSLPassPhraseDialog section.

Certificates

Public key cryptography can be used to digitally sign messages. For example, if you encrypt a message with your secret key, the receiver can guarantee it came from you by simply decrypting it with your public key. But there is a missing step. How can you authenticate people or entities that you have never met in person? In other words, how can you check who a particular public key really belongs to?

The solution involves a trusted third party, the *Certification Authority (CA)*. The CA can be internal to a company or university, or a commercial entity that provides certification services to companies conducting business over the Internet. A CA issues certificates, which are electronic documents that tie a particular public key to information about its owner, such as name and address. The certificates are digitally signed with the CA private key, which certifies that the information is correct.

For this whole process to work, you must trust the CA that issued the certificate. You also need to be able to obtain the public key for that particular CA, which is provided by that CA's so-called root certificate. Most popular browsers, such as Internet Explorer, Firefox, and Safari, bundle a number of root certificates for commonly trusted certification authorities. This allows the browsers to recognize and validate a great number of websites without the user's manual intervention.

Creating a Certificate Signing Request

```
# ./usr/local/ssl/bin/openssl req -new -key
www.example.com.key -out www.example.com.csr
```

To get a certificate issued by a CA, you must first submit what is called a certificate signing request. As explained earlier, the request contains data about the entity requesting the certificate and the public key. This command creates such a request. You will be prompted to provide several pieces of information, as shown in Listing 7.1.

Listing 7.1   Using openssl to Generate a Certificate Request

```
Using configuration from
/usr/local/ssl/openssl/openssl.cnf
Enter PEM pass phrase:
You are about to be asked to enter information that
will be incorporated
into your certificate request.
```

Listing 7.1 **Continued**

```
What you are about to enter is what is called a
Distinguished Name or a DN.
There are quite a few fields but you can leave some
blank
For some fields there will be a default value,
If you enter '.', the field will be left blank.
-----
Country Name (2 letter code) [AU]:US
State or Province Name (full name) [Some-State]:CA
Locality Name (eg, city) []: San Francisco
Organization Name (eg, company) [Internet Widgits
Pty Ltd]:.
Organizational Unit Name (eg, section) []:.
Common Name (eg, YOUR name) []:www.example.com
Email Address []:administrator@example.com
Please enter the following 'extra' attributes
to be sent with your certificate request
A challenge password []:
An optional company name []:
```

It is important that the Common Name field entry matches the address that visitors to your website will type in their browsers. This is one of the checks that the browser will perform for the remote server certificate. If the names differ, a warning indicating the mismatch will be issued to the user.

You can now submit the certificate signing request file with a CA for processing. The exact process will vary for each entity. You can find an extensive list of CAs at http://www.pki-page.org/. Verisign, Thawte, GeoTrust, and Equifax are well-known commercial CAs. There are also a number of community CAs, such as http://www.cacert.org/.

Showing the Contents of a Certificate Signing Request

```
# ./usr/local/ssl/bin/openssl req -noout \
    -text  -in www.example.com.csr
```

Certificate signing requests are stored in a special, compact form. This command will show the contents of the certificate stored in www.example.com.csr in a human-readable form. As mentioned earlier in the chapter, the certificate will contain information about the entity requesting it, the contents of the public key, and a signature made with the private key.

Creating a Self-signed Certificate

In addition to submitting your CSR to a commercial CA, you can always create a self-signed certificate. That is, you can be both the issuer and the subject of the certificate. Although this is not very useful for a commercial website, it will enable you to test your installation of mod_ssl or to have a secure web server while you wait for the official certificate from the CA.

```
# ./usr/local/ssl/bin/openssl x509 -req \
-days 30 -in www.example.com.csr -signkey \
www.example.com.key -out www.example.com.cert
```

You now need to copy your certificate www.example.com.cert (either the one returned by the CA or your self-signed one) to /usr/local/ssl/openssl/certs/ and your key to /usr/local/ssl/openssl/private/.

Protect your key file by issuing the following command:

```
# chmod 400 www.example.com.key
```

Compiling SSL Support in Apache 1.3

```
$ gunzip < mod_ssl-2.8.23-1.3.33.tar.gz | tar xvf -
$ gunzip < apache_1.3.33.tar.gz | tar xvf -
$ cd mod_ssl-2.8.23-1.3.33
$ ./configure --with-apache=../apache_1.3.33
$ cd ../apache_1.3.x
$ SSL_BASE=/usr/local/ssl/ ./configure --enable-mod-
ule=ssl --prefix=/usr/local/apache
$ make
# make install
```

mod_ssl is a very popular module that provides SSL support both for Apache 1.3 and 2.x. Due to historical reasons related to export restrictions on cryptography, the Apache 1.3 version is distributed separately from the server. What is more, the Apache 1.3 source code needs to be patched in order to support mod_ssl. This is done as part of the mod_ssl build process, shown in the previous listing. The example builds Apache 1.3.33 and mod_ssl 2.8.23 and assumes both source directories are located at the same level. The --with-apache command line option points to the location of the Apache 1.3 source code directory, which is later recompiled to include mod_ssl support.

If you are building against the system OpenSSL library, you can remove SSL_BASE=/usr/local/ssl/ from the Apache configure step.

If Apache already contains the EAPI patches and load-able module support, you can use the common APXS build mechanism described in Chapter 1. This is use-ful, for example, when upgrading an existing mod_ssl installation.

If you try to start Apache now, you will get an error stating that it is unable to read the server certificate. Refer to previous sections for details on how to create your server certificate and keys, and to the "Minimal Apache Configuration" section later in the chapter for details on how to bootstrap your server. Optionally, mod_ssl can create a server certificate for testing pur-poses during the build process. To do so, you can do a make certificate before the make install.

Compiling SSL Support in Apache 2.x

Apache 2 was released after the US cryptography export regulations were relaxed, so it includes mod_ssl alongside the rest of the modules.

If you are building Apache from source, you can enable mod_ssl at build time with the --enable-ssl configure option. If you are also building OpenSSL from source, you will need to add --with-ssl=/usr/local/ssl/openssl.

Minimal Apache Configuration

Once you have generated your keys and certificates, either self-signed or certified by a third-party CA, the next step is to configure Apache. As part of the installation process, `mod_ssl` creates a sample SSL configuration. Apache 1.3 adds it to the default `httpd.conf` file and Apache 2.0 includes a separate `ssl.conf` file, referenced by an `Include` directive in `httpd.conf`. The myriad configuration options can be confusing, but in reality there are only a few options that you need to configure, as shown in the following listing:

```
Listen 80
Listen 443
<VirtualHost _default_:443>
ServerName www.example.com
SSLEngine on
SSLCertificateFile \
/usr/local/ssl/openssl/certs/www.example.com.cert
SSLCertificateKeyFile \
/usr/local/ssl/openssl/certs/www.example.com.key
</VirtualHost>
```

One of the `Listen` directives tells Apache to listen at the default HTTPS port, 443. `SSLEngine On` enables SSL for that particular host and the `SSLCertificateFile` and `SSLCertificateKeyFile` directives point to the certificate and private key.

Starting Apache with SSL Support

Once `mod_ssl` has been installed and configured, you can start Apache with

```
apachectl start
```

If you are using the default SSL configuration files, or the ones supplied by your vendor, the SSL directives will likely be surrounded by an `<IfDefine SSL>` block.

You can either remove those blocks or start Apache with

```
apachectl startssl
```

which will pass the -DSSL flag to the server binary and enable the SSL configuration. This only needs to be done in Apache 1.3 and 2.0, as Apache 2.2 no longer includes a startssl option, and SSL directives are not treated any differently than other directives.

If you protected your private key with a pass phrase, you will need to enter it now. If you installed Apache as a regular user, it may have been configured to listen by default at port 8443. As explained in Chapter 2, port 443 is a privileged port and is only accessible by the superuser.

You can test the installation by accessing your server as `https://www.example.com` (or `https://www.example.com:8443` as just explained).

SSLPassPhraseDialog

SSLPassPhraseDialog builtin

If you have password protected your server's private key, you will be asked to provide the appropriate pass phrase at startup time. You can control this behavior with SSLPassPhraseDialog. Its default value, builtin, means that Apache will prompt you directly every time the server is started. You can choose not to protect the key. This is convenient because you will not need to manually enter the pass phrase during reboots, but if the server is compromised, the key will be as well. You can also configure SSLPassPhraseDialog to call an external program, which will provide the pass phrase on its standard input when called from Apache.

```
SSLPassPhraseDialog exec:/usr/local/apache/bin/sslpp
```

If you write the script correctly, this can offer a bit more security than leaving the key unprotected (but not much either).

Improving SSL Performance

The algorithms involved in SSL are CPU-intensive and may slow down your server significantly, especially if you have many simultaneous client connections. The handshake phase can also impose a delay in the request. There are a number of options you can consider to improve the responsiveness of your site.

Make sure you have enabled session caching. This will speed up multiple connections from the same client. If you are using a cluster of SSL servers, you may want to use distcache, so the connection data can be cached even if the client connects to multiple servers in the cluster. Apache 2.2 includes support for distcache out of the box. You can learn more about this project at http://www.distcache.org.

Consider having a dedicated machine just for SSL processing. Depending on your needs, this may be a commercial hardware load balancer or a dedicated machine running a reverse proxy (a web server that relies on requests to other web servers on behalf of the client). This allows for optimizations in the Apache and OS configuration that would not be possible if the machine is also serving other purposes, such as running PHP, Tomcat, and MySQL. A reverse proxy can provide additional benefits such as load-balancing and single sign-on, possibly using client certificates, across a number of backend websites. See Chapter 10 for details.

Finally, you can install a crypto-card, a piece of hardware that is designed to offload the server from performing most of the SSL processing. Apache 2.2 provides support for this functionality; take a look at the SSLCryptoDevice directive.

Forcing All Content to Be Served Using SSL

```
<VirtualHost 192.168.200.4:80>
    ServerName private.example.com
    Redirect / https://private.example.com/
</Virtualhost>
```

If you have a particular website that you want only served under SSL, you can use a Redirect inside a <VirtualHost> container that listens for HTTP requests and redirects them to your secure website, as shown in the example. This is useful because users will not always remember to type https:// instead of http://.

SSL and Name-based SSL Virtual Hosts

A common question from mod_ssl users is whether it is possible to have several SSL-enabled name-based virtual hosts. The short answer is no. The problem is that name-based virtual hosting relies on the information provided by the client in the Host: header of the HTTP request, since all name-based virtual hosts are sharing the same IP address. But the SSL connection takes place at the TCP level, before the HTTP request can be sent. Thus, the server is not able to determine at the time of connection which virtual host the client wants to connect to and, hence, which certificate and key to use. There is indeed a specification (RFC 2817), which allows upgrading an existing HTTP connection to HTTPS. That would get around this issue, but at the time of this writing it is not implemented by any mainstream browser. Apache 2.2's mod_ssl module implements support for RFC 2817, as does mod_nw_ssl, the Netware Apache SSL module.

Using Apache Auth Modules with SSL

```
SSLOptions +FakeBasicAuth
```

When this option is enabled, the Subject Distinguished Name (DN) of the client certificate is translated into an HTTP basic authorization username. This means that the standard Apache authentication methods seen in Chapter 6 can be used for access control. To those authentication modules, it looks as if the user has successfully provided a valid username and password. You will need to modify certain settings in your user databases; see the SSLOptions directive manual page for details.

Warning Messages When Accessing an SSL-enabled Website

Sometimes, when accessing an SSL-enabled website, users get a warning popup window, telling that something is not quite right with the website. These are some of the most common causes:

- The certificate has expired. Commercial certificates are usually valid for a limited period of time, after which they expire.

- The domain in the certificate does not match the domain. This will happen if the certificate was issued for a different website.

- The certificate has been signed by a Certificate Authority that is unknown or not trusted by the browser. This can happen, for example, if you are using a self-signed certificate for testing purposes.

Creating Client Certificates

When using client certificate authorization, the server will verify during the handshake phase that the client presents a valid certificate and that it has been signed by a CA that the server trusts. Although cumbersome to manage and distribute, client certificates are useful for protecting access to company websites or web services. They tend to be more secure than user names and passwords, as they cannot be guessed or intercepted.

If you want to be your own CA, the first step is to create your root CA. You can do so directly using the ca argument to the command line tool, or using the convenient CA.pl wrapper script bundled with openssl. To create a new certificate authority, you can issue the following command:

```
CA.pl -newca
```

The script will now create a private key, server certificate, and so on, and create a directory structure (demoCA) that contains the generated files.

You can now create a CSR and sign your certificate with

```
CA.pl -newreq
CA.pl -signreq
```

The generated CA file will be in PEM format. To convert it to another format that makes it more convenient to import in browsers, execute the following command:

```
CA.pl -pkcs12
```

The exact method to import the certificate in the end-user machine varies depending on the browser type. Internet Explorer users can simply click on the certificate file and follow the instructions.

Authentication Using Client Certificates

```
SSLVerifyClient require
SSLCACertificateFile \
    /usr/local/ssl/openssl/certs/ca.crt
```

Once you have installed certificates in your clients, you need to instruct Apache to enable SSL validation for clients. This `SSLVerifyClient` directive requires clients to provide a valid client certificate to be able to connect. The `SSLCACertificateFile` provides the path to the file containing the trusted CA certificate that will be used to verify the client certificate validity.

Alternatives to `mod_ssl`

There are a number of alternatives to `mod_ssl`. For Apache 1.3, you can use Apache-SSL, the module from which `mod_ssl` originally derived. You can find it at http://www.apache-ssl.org. A number of commercial vendors, such as IBM, include their own SSL modules with their Apache-based web server packages, usually based on toolkits other than OpenSSL.

Finally, you can use a standalone utility, such as `stunnel`, to proxy SSL connections to an existing Apache server as described at http://www.stunnel.org. Though not as flexible as `mod_ssl`, it can be a handy tool for certain scenarios where it is not possible or desirable to modify a running server configuration.

Testing SSL-enabled Websites from the Command Line

```
# openssl s_client -connect www.ibm.com:443
```

You can use `openssl` or other SSL based tools, such as `stunnel` (http://www.stunnel.org), to test secure web servers. For example, you can use this command to connect to IBM's website using HTTPS. It will display details about the SSL protocol and server certificate for the connection. You can then issue a `GET / HTTP/1.0` command and press Enter and get a response back, just as if you had used Telnet to connect to a regular web server on port 80 to issue HTTP requests by hand, as shown in Chapter 1.

Working Around Buggy SSL Implementations

```
SetEnvIf User-Agent ".*MSIE.*" nokeepalive \
    ssl-unclean-shutdown downgrade-1.0 \
force-response-1.0
```

Some browsers (or servers, if operating in a reverse-proxy configuration) have known problems with specific versions of the SSL protocol or certain features. Certain environment variables can be set to force specific behaviors. This is especially useful if you have a commercial site and need to support older browsers. For example, this configuration snippet is included in the default configuration file and is a workaround for bugs in the SSL implementation of Internet Explorer browsers. If the client browser contains the MSIE string then no keep-alive support will be enabled and an earlier version of the HTTP protocol will be used.

Complex Access Control with `mod_ssl`

```
SSLRequire ( %{SSL_CIPHER} !~ m/^(EXP|NULL)-/ \
and %{SSL_CLIENT_S_DN_O} eq "Snake Oil, Ltd." \
and %{SSL_CLIENT_S_DN_OU} in {"Staff", "CA", "Dev"}\
and %{TIME_WDAY} >= 1 and %{TIME_WDAY} <= 5 \
and %{TIME_HOUR} >= 8 and %{TIME_HOUR} <= 20   ) \
or %{REMOTE_ADDR} =~ m/^192\.76\.162\.[0-9]+$/
```

This example shows how to use the SSLRequire directive to implement arbitrary access restrictions based on a number of parameters. As it happens with mod_rewrite, SSLRequire can be complex to configure, but it provides nearly unlimited possibilities. The configuration snippet above checks that

- The SSL connection does not use an export (weak) cipher or a NULL cipher, the certificate has been issued by a particular CA and for a particular group, and the access takes place during workdays (Monday to Friday) and working hours (8:00 a.m. to 8:00 p.m.).

- The client comes from an internal, trusted network (as specified by REMOTE_ADDR).

Please refer to the SSLRequire documentation for in-depth information.

Related Chapters

If you are using Apache as a reverse proxy, SSL-related connection and certificate information for clients is not available to the backend servers. How to solve this issue is discussed in detail in Chapter 10 .

8

Content Publishing with DAV

Content Publishing and Apache

If you are providing hosting for other users, you need an efficient way for them to upload and maintain their websites. This chapter covers the mod_dav module and how to use it to provide users with a way to manage their content. It includes explanations on how to limit write access to particular resources, how to configure different clients (including Windows web folders), and some of the most common issues. It also provides information on how to enable per-user directories so each user can have their own separate web space.

Introducing WebDAV

WebDAV stands for *Web-based Distributed Authoring and Versioning*. It is a protocol that extends HTTP and allows users to remotely upload and modify their content. To appreciate the tremendous usefulness of WebDAV, it is necessary to understand the limitations of pre-existing publishing methods. In the early days of the web, webmasters and system administrators edited the server's content directly from the shell using text editors such as vi or emacs. As the Web grew, different roles emerged: administrators maintaining the server and users and programmers providing the content. It was necessary to have mechanisms in place to allow users to upload and modify their content. This separation of tasks required access restriction policies and easy-to-use methods for updating the website content by non-technical individuals. The tools for generating web content evolved from simple text editors to sophisticated publishing tools, closer to word processors in features and ease of use.

Unfortunately, there was no standard way for those tools and individuals to upload the content. Solutions ranged from allowing users shell access to the system, to using the File Transfer Protocol (FTP) or other proprietary protocols. Shell access requires your users to be familiar with the basics of the Unix command line and comes with all the associated complexity and security issues of allowing direct access to the server. Using an FTP client requires end users to download and install a different tool, and also requires an FTP server. Finally, custom made scripts, file uploads via HTML forms, and proprietary protocols (such as those used by Microsoft FrontPage) raise a number of interoperability and security issues of their own.

WebDAV provides a way around these issues by providing a standard protocol that can be implemented as part of the web server. WebDAV extends the HTTP protocol with new methods for tasks such as creating, deleting, and locking resources for editing. WebDAV is implemented in Apache with mod_dav, which is distributed as a third-party module for Apache 1.3 and as a built-in module for Apache 2.0

Advantages of Using mod_dav

As explained in the previous section, mod_dav is implemented as an Apache module that extends the HTTP protocol. It can take advantage of a number of built-in Apache features, such as SSL for encryption and certificate-based authentication, HTTP basic authentication, proxy servers, and so on. Integration with Apache allows many other possibilities, such as sharing access control mechanisms and interaction with scripting engines such as mod_perl and PHP.

The DAV protocol itself is extensible. Although the resources accessed via DAV usually live in the file system, DAV can act as a standards-based front end to a variety of back-end repositories such as databases, version control systems, and proprietary document management frameworks.

For example, DAV has the concept of collections, which are groups of files. This usually translates to a directory in the server, but it might have a completely different meaning for other back ends.

Finally, WebDAV has been implemented by most modern web publishing frameworks, office suites, and desktop environments.

WebDAV and the HTTP Protocol

DAV is implemented on top of the standard HTTP protocol that allows browsers and web servers to communicate. It extends existing HTTP methods and includes new ones, as described here. You will need this knowledge to implement access control for writing to DAV-enabled resources.

- COPY: Copy files or collections (equivalent to file system directories). Additional headers enable you to specify the recursive copy of nested collections.

- MOVE: Move files and collections.

- MKCOL: Creates a new collection. If parent collections do not exist, an error is raised. Parent collections must be explicitly created using the PUT method.

- PROPFIND: You learned earlier that DAV resources could have metadata information associated with them. The PROPFIND method enables you to query this information.

- PROPPATCH: This method enables you to delete, create, and modify resource metadata.

- LOCK and UNLOCK: These methods allow you to lock a resource. This is useful, for example, for preventing modification to a resource while you are editing it.

The DAV protocol extends existing HTTP methods such as GET and PUT, mainly to make them aware of the new locking features. The OPTIONS method is extended to report DAV capabilities.

Installing mod_dav on Apache 2.0

```
./configure --enable-dav
```

Apache 2.0 bundles mod_dav, although it is not enabled by default. You can enable it as you would do with any other of the included modules. By default, it will also compile the file system back end (--enable-dav-fs). It is also possible to have alternate back ends for DAV, such as the Subversion source management system and databases, as described in Chapter 12.

If you are using the Apache 2 Windows distribution, mod_dav is already present as a DLL, so you will just need to enable the LoadModule directives in the httpd.conf configuration file:

```
LoadModule dav_module modules/mod_dav.so
LoadModule dav_fs_module modules/mod_dav_fs.so
```

Installing mod_dav on Apache 1.3

```
tar xvfz mod_dav-1.0.3-1.3.6.tar.gz
cd mod_dav-1.0.3-1.3.6
./configure --with-apxs=/usr/local/apache/bin/apxs
make
make install
```

Apache 1.3 does not have built-in DAV support. You will need to download and install mod_dav as you would do with any other third-party module, as shown. You can find more information on how to compile third-party modules in Chapter 12. You can download the Unix source code and Windows binaries from http://www.webdav.org/mod_dav/ and http://www.webdav.org/mod_dav/win32/.

Basic WebDAV Configuration

```
DAVLockDB /usr/local/apache/var/DAVLock
<Location />
Dav On
</Location>
```

Configuring DAV is very simple. All you need to do is include DAV on inside the location or directory container you want to make accessible through DAV. The example shows how to DAV-enable your entire website. DAV has its own locking mechanism, and does not rely on the functionality of the underlying file system. You can specify the location of the DAV lock file with the DAVLockDB directive.

There are, however, a few more aspects of DAV configuration that need to be addressed in a production DAV environment: security and interoperability with buggy third-party clients. These are explained in the following sections.

Securing Your WebDAV Configuration

```
<LimitExcept GET HEAD OPTIONS>
    require user davuser
  </LimitExcept>
```

By default, enabling DAV presents a serious security risk. Users will be able to read and modify your web content. This potentially includes the source code for CGI or PHP scripts that may contain sensitive usernames and passwords. It is thus necessary to protect access to DAV-enabled resources. Since DAV is built on top of HTTP, this can be accomplished using standard Apache access-control modules. The example shows how to require a valid username and password for write access to a DAV resource such as MKCOL. This is done using mod_auth, as covered in Chapter 6, and the <LimitExcept> directive.

Listing 8.1   **Protecting DAV Access**

```
<Location />
Dav On
AuthType basic
AuthName "DAV Resource"
AuthUserFile /usr/local/apache2/conf/htusers
<LimitExcept GET HEAD OPTIONS>
    require user davuser
  </LimitExcept>
</Location>
```

<Limit> and <LimitExcept> are two container directives that allow you to apply certain configuration parameters only to specific request methods. While this is not very useful for regular HTTP, it can be very useful for DAV setups. The example allows everyone to access the web content using pure HTTP methods, but restricts DAV access to only authorized users.

There are additional measures you can take, such as running DAV on a separate, single-purpose instance of Apache. This Apache server can run in a separate port and be easily trimmed down and secured. You can also configure it to require SSL or IP-based access control for additional protection.

Accessing DAV Resources from Microsoft Office

Recent versions of Microsoft Office, such as Office 2000 and Office XP, enable you to open and edit documents directly from DAV-enabled servers, including recent versions of Exchange. You can simply specify a URL for a DAV-enabled location in the Open dialog of the application or use the add a new network place dialog, as shown in Figure 8.1. Once that is done, this will allow you to easily create, edit, and share documents in the remote server.

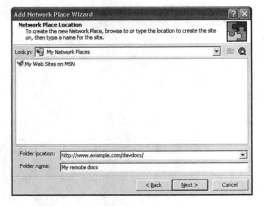

Figure 8.1 Adding a network place in Microsoft Office.

Accessing DAV from Microsoft Windows

Recent versions of Microsoft operating systems, such as Windows 2000 and Windows XP, provide support for DAV via web folders. Web folders allow transparent access to DAV-enabled servers by presenting them as Windows desktop folders. Windows users can then drag and drop files into these folders, double-click to edit them, and so on. You can access a DAV resource as a web folder on a Windows 2000 machine directly from Explorer or by using a wizard.

The rest of this section assumes an Apache server serving the www.example.com domain with DAV-support enabled under the /davdocs section of the website. Make sure the appropriate RedirectCarefully directive is in place, as explained later in the "Dealing with Buggy Clients" section.

Open an Internet Explorer window. Click on the File menu entry and select Open. A pop-up window will appear, as shown in Figure 8.2.

Figure 8.2 Opening a DAV resource from Explorer.

Type the following URL: http://www.example.com/davdocs/. Check the Open as Web Folder option and click OK. Explorer will connect to the resource, and you should now be able to create directories, drag and drop files, and edit them as shown in Figure 8.3.

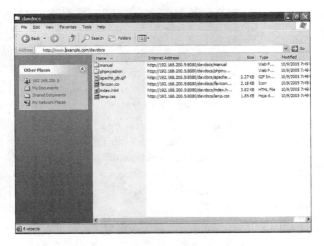

Figure 8.3 View of a DAV resource.

The location will be added automatically to the My Network Places folder. You can access this folder by clicking the desktop icon with the same name.

You can also add a web folder using a wizard by first going to the My Network Places folder mentioned in the previous section and then clicking on the Add Network Place icon and following the onscreen instructions.

Accessing DAV Resources from Firefox

At the time of the writing of this book, Firefox does not include native support for accessing DAV resources. However, the Windows-only `openwebfolder` extension allows you to hook into the Microsoft Windows WebDAV component, allowing you to access DAV resources from within Firefox. It is available from http://openwebfolder.mozdev.org/.

To install it, just click on the XPI link at http://open-webdev.mozdev.org/installation.html from within Firefox and follow the instructions. Once you have restarted Firefox, you can right-click any page and select Open as Web Folder from the pop-up to access it through WebDAV (see Figure 8.4).

Figure 8.4   Open a web folder from inside Firefox.

Accessing DAV from the Command Line

```
./cadaver
dav:!> open http://example.com
```

There are a number of command-line clients available to access DAV-enabled resources, allowing both for interactivity and easy integration within administrative scripts. They can be convenient replacements for their FTP and scp counterparts. Two of the most popular open source command-line clients are cadaver and sitecopy. cadaver is an interactive shell that provides FTP-style commands such as ls, put, get, and so on. The example shows how to use cadaver to access a DAV-enabled web server, list the available resources, and edit a remote file.

```
./cadaver
dav:!> open http://example.com
dav:/> ls
Listing collection `/': succeeded.
Coll:   images                         0
Dec  7 2004
Coll:   styles                         0
Dec 12 2004
        Home.html                   4816
Aug 14 14:19
        company.html                5352
Dec  7 2004
        partners.html               6087
Dec  7 2004
        solutions.html              3037
Dec  7 2004
dav:/> edit solutions.html
Locking `solutions.html': succeeded.
```

```
Downloading `/solutions.html' to /tmp/cadaver-edit-
zEzdL9.html
Progress: [=============================>] 100.0% of
6230 bytes succeeded.
Running editor: `vi /tmp/cadaver-edit-
zEzdL9.html'...
Changes were made.
Uploading changes to `/solutions.html'
Progress: [=============================>] 100.0% of
6232 bytes succeeded.
Unlocking `solutions.html': succeeded.
dav:/>
```

cadaver can be downloaded from http://www.web-
dav.org/cadaver. sitecopy allows you to maintain a
local document tree and a remote server synchronized
using a variety of protocols, including DAV. It can be
downloaded from http://www.lyra.org/sitecopy.

Dealing with Buggy Clients

```
BrowserMatch "Microsoft Data Access Internet
Publishing Provider" redirect-carefully
BrowserMatch "^gnome-vfs" redirect-carefully
```

If you can't connect to your DAV server using
Microsoft web folders or older versions of Gnome virtual folders and you find something similar to

```
"OPTIONS /davdocs HTTP/1.1" 301
```

in your access log, you have hit a bug with certain
client implementations of WebDAV. Apache is sending
a redirect (HTTP code 301) to the client, but the
client is getting confused and does not follow the redirect. Apache provides a workaround against this buggy

behavior, skipping the redirect when the `redirect-carefully` environment variable is set. This example, included in the default Apache configuration file, sets the `redirect-carefully` environment variable for two WebDAV clients known to have the problems mentioned.

mod_speling and DAV

If you are using DAV, you will need to disable `mod_speling`. This is required, as `mod_speling` will interfere with a number of DAV-related operations, such as creating new resources, by erroneously matching them to existing files if the names are similar. `mod_speling` is used to correct user spelling mistakes and is described in Chapter 4.

Dynamic Content and DAV

```
Alias /php /usr/local/apache/php_files
Alias /php-source /usr/local/apache/php_files
<Location /php-source>
    DAV On
    ForceType text/plain
</Location>
```

When accessing resources that are dynamically generated, such as PHP pages or CGI scripts, you may run into a problem where Apache returns the dynamically generated content and not the source code for the file. In other words, you get the contents of the file after it has been processed by the web server and not the source code. To get around this, you can run a separate web server or virtual host that does not have PHP support enabled, as described in an earlier section.

Another method is to map the same file system path to different URLs and selectively enable or disable modules. The example, taken from the DAV documentation, shows how to do just that. It forces all content served through the /php-source URL to be of type text/plain, thus bypassing execution by the PHP engine.

Enabling Per-user Pages

```
UserDir enabled
UserDir public_html
```

Have you ever accessed an URL similar to http://www.example.com/~joe?

That is what is called a per-user web page. Each user in the system is assigned a URL that starts with ~ and the name of the user. When Apache finds such a request, it maps it to a special path inside the user's home directory. This functionality allows each one of your users to publish their own content. This functionality is provided by mod_userdir. You can enable and disable this functionality with the UserDir enabled and UserDir disabled configuration directives. You can also specify an additional list of usernames to selectively enable or disable, as in UserDir disabled mysql root.

If the first argument is not enabled or disabled, it is used to specify where per-user websites are stored. For example, UserDir public_html will map a request for http://www.example.com/~user/ to /home/user/public_html/. The path itself can also contain a pattern, such as

```
UserDir /home/*/web
```

which will map http://www.example.com/~user/
index.thml to

/home/user/web/index.html

The per-user directories need to be readable by the
user Apache runs as. Finally, you can choose to redirect
the client to a certain URL. For example

UserDir http://www.example.com

will map http://www.example.com/~user/index.thml to

http://www.example/user/index.html.

Alternate User Directories

```
RewriteEngine On
RewriteCond %{HTTP_HOST} !^(www\.)
RewriteCond %{HTTP_HOST} ^([^.]+)\.example\.com
RewriteRule ^(.*)$  /home/%1/public_html$1
```

If you do not want to enable mod_dir, or you need a
slightly different functionality than it offers, you may
want to consider using mod_vhost_alias or
mod_rewrite. The example shows how to use
mod_rewrite to map requests for user.example.com to
the appropriate per-user html directory.

Fixing Problems with DAVLockDB

```
No such file or directory: A lock database was not
specified with the DAVLockDB directive. One must be
specified to use the locking functionality. [500,
#401]
```

If you find a message similar to this, it means that you need to provide a DavLockDB directive in the configuration file, as shown:

```
DAVLockDB /usr/local/apache/var/DAVLock
```

If the directive is specified, but the directory containing the lock file cannot be written to, you will get a message similar to the following:

```
The lock database could not be opened, preventing
access to the various lock properties for the
PROPFIND. [500, #0]
```

Fix the permissions so the path of the DavLockDB directive has write permission for the user Apache runs as.

Performance and Scalability

Tuning Apache

This chapter explains which configuration options can affect performance and scalability in Apache, and how to tune them. The good news is that, in most cases, it will not be necessary. Most scalability and speed issues are likely to come from the dynamic content generation engine and database layer, not from the Apache web server. Some of the problems and solutions discussed in this chapter are generic enough that they apply to most server software, while others are Apache-specific.

Understanding Performance and Scalability

Improving the performance and scalability of any computer system involves a mixture of experience, profiling work, and understanding of the server's inner workings. This chapter provides a number of bite-sized suggestions and ideas that will help you get started. For the sake of simplicity, *performance* refers to serving requests faster and *scalability* refers to being able to serve a great number of requests simultaneously.

Tuning Your Hardware

```
vmstat
```

Likely, the single most important action that you can take to improve the performance of your server is to increase the amount of RAM. That extra RAM will allow the operating system to cache frequently accessed disk files, as well as to support multiple Apache children running simultaneously.

The second aspect to consider is disk speed. Fast disks with large amounts of onboard cache can significantly improve the load. You may also want to modify different drive parameters, such as enabling Direct Memory Access support for your drive. Under Linux, you can achieve this with the hdparm utility.

vmstat is a useful Unix tool for finding bottlenecks. This tool reports information about processes, memory, paging, block IO, traps, and CPU activity.

If you are using SSL in your server and need to support many simultaneous users, that can require a lot of CPU resources. A faster processor or a dedicated crypto card will help in this situation. Please refer to Chapter 7 and to the improving SSL performance section in Chapter 10 for additional settings that can help. Finally, machines with multiple CPUs and/or multicore CPUs greatly increase the scalability of process-based web servers and are recommended for medium- and heavy-duty hosting.

Increasing OS Limits

`ulimit`

Several operating system factors can prevent Apache from scaling. These factors are related to process creation, memory limits, and maximum simultaneous number of open files or connections.

The Unix `ulimit` command enables you to set several of the limits covered in the next few sections on a per-process basis. Please refer to your operating system documentation for details on `ulimit`'s syntax.

Increasing OS Limits on Processes

Apache provides settings for preventing the number of server processes and threads from exceeding certain limits. These settings affect scalability because they limit the number of simultaneous connections to the web server, which in turn affects the number of visitors that you can service simultaneously. These settings vary from MPM to MPM and are described in detail in Chapter 11.

The Apache MPM settings are in turn constrained by OS settings limiting the number of processes and threads. The steps needed to change the limits vary from operating system to operating system. In Linux 2.4 and 2.6 kernels, the limit can be accessed and set at runtime by editing the /proc/sys/kernel/threads-max file. You can read the contents of the file with

```
cat /proc/sys/kernel/threads-max
```

and write to it using

```
echo value > /proc/sys/kernel/threads-max
```

In Linux (unlike most other Unix versions), there is a mapping between threads and processes, and they are similar from the point of view of the OS. In Solaris, those parameters can be changed in the /etc/system file. Such changes don't require rebuilding the kernel, but might require a reboot to take effect. You can change the total number of processes by changing the max_nprocs entry and the number of processes allowed for a given user with maxuproc.

Increasing OS File Descriptors

Whenever a process opens a file (or a socket), a structure called a file descriptor is assigned until the file is closed. The OS limits the number of file descriptors that a given process can open, thus limiting the number of simultaneous connections the web server can have. How those settings are changed depends on the operating system. On Linux systems, you can read or modify /proc/sys/fs/file-max (using echo and cat as explained in the previous section). On Solaris systems, you must edit the value for rlim_fd_max in the /etc/system file. This change will require a reboot to take effect.

You can find additional information at http://httpd.apache.org/docs/misc/descriptors.html.

Controlling External Processes

```
RlimitCPU
RLimitMem
RLimitNProc
```

Apache provides several directives to control the amount of resources that external processes use. This applies to CGI scripts spawned from the server and programs executed via Server Side Includes. Support for the following directives is available only on Unix and varies from system to system:

- RLimitCPU: Accepts two parameters—the soft limit and the hard limit for the amount of CPU time in seconds that a process is allowed. If the max keyword is used, it indicates the maximum setting allowed by the operating system. The hard limit is optional. The soft limit can be changed between restarts, and the hard limit specifies the maximum allowed value for that setting. If you are confused, check Chapter 11 for a similar discussion with ServerLimit and MaxClients.

- RLimitMem: The syntax is identical to RLimitCPU but this directive specifies the amount (in bytes) of memory used per process.

- RLimitNProc: The syntax is identical to RLimitCPU but this directive specifies the number of processes.

These three directives are useful to prevent malicious or poorly written programs from running out of control.

Improving File System Performance

Accessing the disk is an expensive operation in terms of resources and is one of the slowing factors for any server. If you can cut the number of times Apache or the operating system need to read from disk or write to disk, performance can be improved significantly. The following sections discuss some of the parameters you can fine tune to achieve this. In addition, most modern operating systems are very efficient with filesystem caching, and thus ensuring that enough RAM is available can also dramatically improve file access speed for commonly accessed files.

Mounting File Systems with noatime Option

Many Linux file systems can be mounted with the noatime option. This means that the operating system will not record the last time a file was accessed when reading it, though it will still keep track of the last time it was written to. This can provide significant speed improvements, especially in heavily loaded servers. The following line shows a sample /etc/fstab entry:

```
/dev/hda3    /www    ext2    defaults,noatime    1  1
```

Handling Symbolic Links

```
Options FollowSymLinks
```

In Unix, a symbolic link (or symlink) is a special kind of file that points to another file. It is created with the

Unix `ln` command and is useful for making a certain file appear in different places.

Two of the parameters that the `Options` directive allows are `FollowSymLinks` and `SymLinksIfOwnerMatch`. By default, Apache won't follow symbolic links because they can be used to bypass security settings and provide unwanted access to parts of your filesystem. For example, you can create a symbolic link from a public part of the website to a restricted file or directory not otherwise accessible via the Web. So, also by default, Apache needs to perform a check to verify that the file isn't a symbolic link. If `SymLinksIfOwnerMatch` is present, it will follow a symbolic link if the target file is owned by the same user who created the symbolic link. Because those tests must be performed for every path element and for every path that refers to a file system object, they can be expensive. If you control the content creation, you should add an `Options +FollowSymLinks` directive to your configuration and avoid the `SymLinksIfOwnerMatch` argument. In this way, the tests won't take place and performance isn't affected.

Disabling Per-directory Configuration Files

```
<Directory />
AllowOverride none
</Directory>
```

As explained in previous chapters, per-directory configuration files provide a convenient way of configuring the server and allow for some degree of delegated administration. However, if this feature is enabled, Apache has to look for these files in each directory in

the path leading to the document being served. You
can disable this feature by adding AllowOverride none
to your configuration.

Configuring Content Negotiation

As explained in the "Configuring Content
Negotiation" section in Chapter 4, Apache can serve
different versions of a file depending on client language or preferences. This can be accomplished with
file extensions, but for every request, Apache must
access the file system repeatedly looking for files with
appropriate extensions. If you need to use content
negotiation, make sure that you at least use a type-map
file, minimizing accesses to disk.

Disabling or Minimizing Logging

```
BufferedLogs On
```

In heavily loaded websites, logging can slow down the
server significantly. You can minimize its impact by not
logging hits to all or certain images (such as naviga-
tional buttons). Additionally, you can buffer logs before
they are written to disk using the BufferedLogs directive included in mod_log_config in Apache 2 and later.
Finally, you can decide to use modules such as
mod_log_spread that allow you to log to the network
instead of to local disk, improving performance. You
can download this module from http://www.
backhand.org/mod_log_spread.

Tuning Network and Status Settings

A number of network-related Apache settings can degrade performance. The following sections discuss some of the most relevant.

HostnameLookups

```
HostnameLookups off
```

When `HostnameLookups` is set to on or `double`, Apache will perform a DNS lookup to capture the hostname of the client, introducing a delay in the response to the client. The default setting is `HostnameLookups off`. If you need to use the hostnames, you can always process the request logs with a log resolver later, as explained in Chapter 3.

Certain other settings can trigger a DNS lookup, even if `HostnameLookups` is set to off, such as when a hostname is used in `Allow` or `Deny` rules, as covered in Chapter 6.

Request Accept Mechanism

Apache can use different mechanisms to control how Apache children arbitrate requests. The optimal mechanism depends on the specific platform and number of processors. Additional information can be found at http://httpd.apache.org/docs/2.0/misc/perf-tuning.html.

mod_status

This module collects statistics about the server, connections, and requests. Although this can be useful to troubleshoot Apache, it can also slow down the server. For optimal performance, disable this module, or at least make sure that ExtendedStatus is set to off, which is the default.

AcceptFilter

```
AcceptFilter http data
AcceptFilter https data
```

A number of operating systems, such as Linux and FreeBSD, allow you to mark certain listening sockets as handling specific protocols. Thus, it is possible to ask the kernel to only pass a request to Apache once all the content of the HTTP request has been received, improving performance. This capability is only implemented in Apache 2.1 and later, although there is an earlier, BSD-specific version of the AcceptFilter directive present in Apache 1.3.22 and later. You can find more in-depth documentation for socket configuration in the AcceptFilter manual page.

KeepAlives

```
KeepAlive On
KeepAliveTimeout 5
MaxKeepAliveRequests 500
```

HTTP 1.1 allows multiple requests to be served over a single connection. HTTP 1.0 allows the same thing with keep-alive extensions. The KeepAliveTimeout directive enables you to specify the maximum time in seconds that the server will wait before closing an inactive connection. Increasing the timeout means that you will increase the chance of the connection being reused. On the other hand, it also ties up the connection and Apache process during the waiting time, which can prevent scalability, as discussed earlier. The MaxKeepAliveRequest directive allows you to specify the maximum amount of times the connection will be reused.

Preventing Abuse

```
TimeOut
LimitRequestBody
LimitRequestFields
LimitRequestFieldSize
LimitRequestLine
LimitXMLRequestBody
```

Denial of service (DoS) attacks work by swamping your site with a great number of simultaneous requests, slowing down the server or preventing access altogether to legitimate clients. DoS attacks are difficult to prevent in general, and usually the most effective way to address them is at the network or operating system level. One example is blocking specific addresses from making requests to the server; although you can block those addresses at the web server level, it is more efficient to block them at the network firewall/router or with the operating system network filters.

Other kinds of abuse include posting extremely big requests or opening a great number of simultaneous connections. You can limit the size of requests and timeouts to minimize the effect of attacks. The default request timeout is 300 seconds, but you can change it with the `TimeOut` directive. A number of directives enable you to control the size of the request body and headers: `LimitRequestBody`, `LimitRequestFields`, `LimitRequestFieldSize`, `LimitRequestLine`, and `LimitXMLRequestBody`.

Limiting Connections and Bandwidth

If you are providing hosting services for several clients, you may face the situation where one of your clients' websites is degrading the performance of the service as a whole. This may be because the website was linked from a high traffic news page (the so-called "Slashdot effect") or because it is hosting a popular set of music or video files. There are a number of Apache modules that allow you to measure and control bandwidth and number of connections, to make sure the impact on other customers and the server as a whole is kept to a minimum. Throttling in this context usually means slowing down the delivery of content based on the file requested, a specific client IP address, the number of simultaneous requests, and so on.

The `mod_bandwidth` Apache 1.3 module enables the setting of server-wide or per-connection bandwidth limits, based on the specific directory, size of files, and remote IP/domain.

http://www.cohprog.com/mod_bandwidth.html

The `bandwidth share` module provides bandwidth throttling and balancing by client IP address. It supports Apache 1.3 and earlier versions of Apache 2.

http://www.topology.org/src/bwshare/
README.html

The `mod_throttle` module throttles bandwidth per virtual host or user, for Apache 1.3.

http://www.snert.com/Software/mod_throttle/
index.shtml

The `Robotcop` module helps you prevent spiders from accessing parts of their sites they have marked off limits.

http://www.robotcop.org/

`mod_require_host` allows you to restrict access to those clients (such as many IIS worms) that do not provide a host header and just try to connect to your IP address

http://www.snert.com/Software/mod_require_host/
index.shtml

`mod_choke` is a module for Apache that limits usage by the number of concurrent connections per IP, and limits the rate at which apache sends data to the client.

http://os.cyberheatinc.com/modules.php?name=
Content&pa=showpage&pid=7

`mod_tsunami` allows you to limit the number of Apache children per virtual host.

http://sourceforge.net/projects/mod-tsunami/

Dealing with Robots

http://www.robotstxt.org/

Robots, web spiders, and web crawlers are names that define a category of programs that download pages from your website, recursively following your site's links. Web search engines use these programs to scan the Internet for web servers, download their content, and index it. Normal users use them to download an entire website or portion of a website for later offline browsing. Normally these programs are well behaved, but sometimes they can be very aggressive and swamp your website with too many simultaneous connections or become caught in cyclic loops.

Well-behaved spiders will request a special file, called robots.txt, that contains instructions about how to access your website and which parts of the website won't be available to them.

The syntax for the file can be found at http://www.robotstxt.org. You can stop the requests at the router or operating system levels.

But sometimes web spiders don't honor the robots.txt file. In those cases, you can use the `Robotcop` Apache module mentioned in the previous section, which enables you to stop misbehaving robots.

Reverse Proxies and Load Balancers

```
mod_proxy_http
mod_backhand http://www.backhand.org/mod_backhand/
```

So far we have covered vertical scalability, which deals with how to improve the performance of a single server configuration. Distributing the load across multiple web servers is horizontal scalability. In this set of architectures, you can expand your capacity by simply adding new machines, improving the amount of traffic you can serve as well as the reliability of your setup.

Chapter 10 deals with using Apache as a reverse proxy. In this setup, one or several lightweight front-end servers deal with static content and handling SSL requests and slow connections, while relaying requests for specific URLs to specialized back-end servers. A number of companies provide commercial products that implement this functionality using hardware appliances.

Finally, mod_backhand is an Apache 1.3 module that provides dynamic redirection of HTTP requests within a cluster of machines, based on available resources.

Caching and Compression

The fastest way to serve content is to not serve it! This can be achieved by using appropriate HTTP headers that instruct clients and proxies of the validity in time of the requested resources. In this way, some resources that appear in multiple pages but don't change frequently, such as logos or navigation buttons, are transmitted only once for a certain period of time.

Additionally, you can use mod_cache (described in Chapter 10) to cache dynamic content so that it doesn't need to be created for every request. This is potentially a big performance boost because dynamic content usually requires accessing databases, processing templates, and so on, which can take significant resources.

Another way to reduce the load on the servers is to reduce the amount of data being transferred to the client. This, in turn, makes your clients' website access faster, especially for those over slow links. To help with this, you can reduce the number and size of your images. You can automate part of this process using the ImageMagick command-line tools (http://www. imagemagick.org). Additionally, you can compress big downloadable files or even static HTML files and use content negotiation, as described in previous chapters. Chapter 11 explains how to use the mod_deflate filtering module to compress HTML content. This can be useful if CPU power is available and clients are connecting over slow links. The content will be delivered faster and the process will be free sooner to answer additional requests.

Module-specific Optimizations

As mentioned at the beginning of the chapter, most bottlenecks occur at the content-generation and database access layers. There are a certain number of modules that can help.

For example, FastCGI and mod_perl can be used to speed up CGI script execution, as explained in "Improving CGI Script Performance" in Chapter 4, and a number of encoders and optimizers exist for PHP, the most popular web development language that runs on Apache, as explained in Chapter 12.

Alternatives to Apache

- lighttpd: http://www.lighttpd.net/
- thttpd: http://www.acme.com/software/thttpd/
- Boa: http://www.boa.org

Apache is a portable, secure, extremely flexible web server. Precisely because of that, it is not necessarily the best solution for all scenarios. The servers mentioned here are optimized, lightweight web servers that often perform or scale better than Apache for certain tasks. For example, some popular websites such as Slashdot use Apache running `mod_perl` to generate content and a different server such as Boa to serve static images files. This is easily accomplished by serving the images from a different domain, such as images.slashdot.org.

Some of the projects also include other popular Apache features, such as URL rewriting and PHP support.

Apache Proxy and Caching Support

Understanding the Need for Caching and Proxies

HTTP is a very simple, yet powerful, protocol. This chapter explains how to take advantage of caching and proxying features that allow you to implement scalable, flexible architectures. Caching allows you to simultaneously reduce the load on your servers and allow faster access to your site by quickly returning frequently requested content. Proxying allows you to create a control point for HTTP requests, which may be used to unify content from various backend servers as well as improving performance.

Understanding Forward and Reverse Proxies

There are different kinds of web proxies. A traditional HTTP proxy, also called a forward proxy, accepts requests from clients (usually web browsers), contacts the remote server, and returns the responses.

A reverse proxy is a web server that is placed in front of other servers, providing a unified frontend and acting as a gateway. As far as the web browsers are concerned, the reverse proxy is the "real" server, as that is the only one they interact with. The reverse proxy relays requests as necessary to the backend servers.

Differences Between Apache 1.3, 2.0, and 2.2

In Apache 1.3, caching support was part of mod_proxy and could not be used separately. In 2.0, the functionality was split into two separate modules, although the resulting code was considered experimental. This changed in 2.1 and 2.2, where the functionality is finally considered mature.

Enabling mod_proxy Support

Apache 1.3

```
--enable-module=proxy
```

Apache 2

```
--enable-proxy
--enable-proxy-connect
--enable-proxy-ftp
--enable-proxy-http
--enable-proxy-balancer (apache 2.1 and later)
--enable-proxy-ajp (apache 2.1 and later)
```

To enable proxy support in Apache, you need to enable the main proxy module and some or all of the three supported backends: HTTP, CONNECT, and FTP. The CONNECT option allows SSL connections to pass untouched via the proxy. The FTP backend allows the proxy server to act as a gateway to access remote FTP servers via a normal HTTP browser. Apache 2.1 and later versions include two additional proxy modules: balancer, which provides load-balancing support, and ajp, which provides support for the AJP protocol, commonly used to communicate with Tomcat and other servlet engines.

Enabling Forward Proxy Support

```
ProxyRequests on
<Proxy *>
Order deny,allow
Deny from all
Allow from 10.0.0.0/255.255.255.0
</Proxy>
```

Forward proxies were popular in the early days of the Internet, as they allowed several machines to easily share a connection to the outside world. Most proxy servers also include caching features, which proves useful when sharing slow connections, as well as offering isolation from the outside world. Fast connections and built-in NAT (Network Address Translation) in most gateway devices have significantly reduced the need for forward proxies. Nowadays, they are most commonly implemented when organizations need to control their employee's browsing, using the proxy to log, filter, and authorize access to websites. This is starting to change, and as spyware and viruses become more common, organizations are implementing filtering proxies that remove these threats before they arrive to the user's desktop. Proxies have thus found new life in the wireless network world as gateways.

You can enable forward proxy functionality using `ProxyRequests On`, as shown in the example. It is a good idea to restrict proxy support to only authorized clients, for the reasons explained in Chapter 6, "Security and Access Control." You can do so using the `<Proxy>` container directive. The example shows how to restrict proxy access to a specific network space.

Using a Reverse Proxy to Unify Your URL Space

```
ProxyPass /crm http://crm.example.com/
ProxyPass /bugzilla
    http://backend.example.com/bugzilla
```

A reverse proxy can provide a unified frontend to a number of backend resources, associating certain URLs on the frontend machine to specific backend web servers. For example, you may have one server running a CRM application and another one running a bug tracking tool. Whenever your users need to use one application, they need to type a different address. You could integrate these services with your main site using ProxyPass, as shown in the example.

Now, when the reverse proxy machine receives a request for http://www.example.com/crm/login/index.html, it will request http://crm.example.com/login/index.html from the backend server and return the document to the browser.

The ProxyPass directive can be used standalone or inside a <Location> container, as in the following example:

```
<Location /crm>
ProxyPass http://crm.example.com/
</Location>
```

Finally, you probably want to use ProxyPass together with ProxyPassReverse, described in the following section.

Hiding the Backend Servers

```
ProxyPass /crm http://crm.example.com
ProxyPassReverse /crm http://crm.example.com
ProxyErrorOverride On
```

During the process described in the previous section, the client has only contacted the reverse proxy server and is unaware of the existence of the backend servers. Sometimes, however, the backend server will issue redirects or error pages that contain references to itself, for example in the Location: header.

The ProxyPassReverse directive will intercept these headers and rewrite them so that they include a reference to the reverse proxy (www.example.com) instead. The ProxyPassReverseCookiePath and

ProxyPassReverseCookieDomain directives operate similarly, but on the path and domain strings in Set-Cookie: headers.

Additionally, ProxyErrorOverride, which is only available in Apache 2, will allow you to display the error pages of the proxy server, replacing the error pages received from the backend. This enables you to further hide the existence of that backend server and provide a consistent frontend, even for error messages.

NOTE: Note that the ProxyPassReverse directive operates only at the HTTP header level. It will not inspect or rewrite links inside HTML documents. For that purpose, you can use mod_proxy_html, an Apache 2 module that allows you to parse the documents being served through the proxy and rewrite the HTML on the fly. You can download it from http://apache.webthing.com/mod_proxy_html/.

Preventing URLs from Being Reverse Proxied

```
ProxyPass /images/ !
ProxyPass / http://crm.example.com
```

It is possible to prevent certain URLs from not being proxied by specifying an exclamation mark (!) as the remote site URL in ProxyPass directives. It is important that those directives be placed before other ProxyPass directives. For example, this configuration will pass all requests to a backend site, except requests for images, which will be served locally.

Improving Performance

```
ProxyIOBufferSize 1024000
```

Reverse proxies can also be useful when you have complex, overloaded web and application servers. Slow clients over modem lines, buggy browsers, and big multimedia files can tie up valuable resources in the servers creating the content. If a client requests a big static file and downloads it slowly, an Apache child process or thread will be busy serving it until the download completes. A similar scenario occurs when some buggy TCP/IP implementations fail to properly close a connection to the server after the transmission has finished. This is called the "lingering close" problem and will cause resources to be tied up until the connection is closed because of a timeout. While these issues are hardly avoidable, the real problem occurs when you are using process-based MPMs (such as the prefork MPM). For example, if you are running mod_perl in Apache 1.3 with multiple other Perl modules loaded and some cached data, the resulting Apache children will likely be several megabytes in size. Whenever one of them is "wasting time" serving static files or waiting for a connection to close, there are less system resources available to serve the remaining requests. A reverse proxy can help here. You can have one or several threaded, lightweight Apache frontends serving your static content and taking care of slow and buggy clients and backend, full-featured, servers doing the dynamic content generation. You can tune ProxyIOBufferSize so big files are transferred to the reverse proxy quickly and the connection to the back-end server is freed as soon as possible. This reduces the load on the backend server, though it increases the memory consumption in the proxy machine. Recent MPMs in Apache 2.1 allow the same Apache child to manage multiple connections, including having a dedicated thread whose task is to wait for connections to close. These MPMs, as they mature, will allow Apache to scale much better in a number of situations.

Offloading SSL Processing

As seen in Chapter 7, "SSL/TLS," the computations required make SSL a resource-intensive protocol. This may impact the performance of your backend servers in a similar way to what was described in the previous section. One way to solve this issue is by having dedicated, optimized boxes running a reverse proxy with SSL support. The reverse proxy does all the heavy lifting, processing the SSL requests, maybe doing certificate-based authentication, and passing the requests as plain HTTP to the backend servers. The content is generated and returned to the reverse proxy, which performs the resource-intensive task of encrypting it. Since the SSL end-point is the reverse proxy, some information, such as certificate-related information, is lost and does not reach the backend server. How to do this is described in the next couple of sections.

Passing Proxy Information in Headers

`ProxyPreserveHost on`

When Apache is acting as a reverse proxy, the Host: header is modified in the proxy request to match the hostname specified in the ProxyPass directive. The original `Host:` header is placed in another header, `X-Forwarded-Host`. In certain situations, it is desirable to preserve the original value of the header. This can be done by setting `ProxyPreserveHost on` in the configuration file.

Certain information about the request gets lost when a reverse proxy is in place. The reverse proxy records some of that information in new headers that are added to the request to the backend server:

- `X-Forwarded-For:` IP address or hostname of the client
- `X-Forwarded-Host:` Original host requested
- `X-Forwarded-Server:` Hostname for the proxy server

You can pass additional information using the `Header` and `RequestHeader` directives, as shown in the next section.

Manipulating Headers

Header set header-name header-value

You can pass additional information to a backend server using the `Header` directive, provided by the `mod_headers` module. This module can be used to add and remove arbitrary headers in HTTP requests and responses.

You can add a response HTTP header, deleting any other HTTP headers with the same name that might be present by using `Header set`, as shown in the example. If you want to add a new header instead of replacing an existing one, you can use `Header add` instead of `Header set`. If you want to append the value to an existing header, remove certain headers, or add a request header to the response, you can use append, unset, and echo respectively.

You can modify the request headers sent to the client by using RequestHeader instead of Header. You can add the content of environment variables to the header-value argument by using the format string %{variable-name}e. This is similar to how the LogFormat directive works, as explained in Chapter 3, "Logs and Monitoring." For example, you can use this to pass information about an SSL connection and certificates to the backend server. For that, you will need first to tell mod_ssl to store this information in environment variables with SSLOptions +StdEnvVars. Starting with Apache 2.1, you can avoid that step and access SSL environment variables directly with %{variable-name}s.

Implementing a Caching Proxy

```
CacheRoot /usr/local/apache/cache
CacheSize 500000
CacheGcInterval 6
CacheMaxExpire 12
```

One of the advantages of a proxy is that it can cache the information that it serves. The next time that the same content is requested, the proxy can check whether it is already present in the cache and, if so, serve it directly from there. In Apache 1.3, the caching functionality is implemented as part of the mod_proxy module. These directives represent a sample configuration. CacheRoot allows you to specify the location of the cached files and CacheSize allows you to set the overall size in kilobytes of the cache. There are a number of other configuration directives that you can use to tweak the caching behavior. `CacheGcInterval` allows you to specify the frequency in hours that the cache will be periodically "purged" to comply with the `CacheSize` setting. `CacheMaxExpire` specifies the maximum amount of time a document can remain in the cache and still be considered valid without having to check with the original source.

Caching in Apache 2

```
CacheEnable disk /
CacheRoot /usr/local/apache/cache
```

The caching and proxying functionality in Apache was split into separate modules starting with Apache 2. While in Apache 2.0 the caching functionality is considered experimental, it is considered of production quality in Apache 2.1/2.2

In Apache 2, the main caching functionality is implemented by `mod_cache`, which in turn has two backends: `mod_mem_cache`, which stores cached resources directly in memory, and `mod_disk_cache`, which uses the file system. The `CacheEnable` directive takes a caching backend (`mem` or `disk`) parameter and a URL prefix. Requests that contain the URL prefix will be cached by the specified backend. You can use `CacheDisable` to disable caching for specific URLs. You can use the `htcacheclean` command-line utility to prune the cache at predefined intervals when using the `disk` backend.

Alternatively, if you have frequently requested files that you know will not change during the life of the server, you can use `mod_file_cache` to tell Apache to map specific files into memory or cache file handles:

```
CacheFile /usr/local/apache/htdocs/navigationbar.gif
MMapFile /usr/local/apache/htdocs/button_left.png
```

If you modify any of the static files, you will need to restart the server for the changes to take effect.

Load Balancing

```
<Location /balancer-manager>
SetHandler balancer-manager
Order deny,allow
Deny from all
Allow from localhost
</Location>
<Proxy balancer://balancer/ stickysession=PHPSES-
SIONID>
BalancerMember http://www1.example.com/
BalancerMember http://www2.example.com/
BalancerMember http://www3.example.com/
</Proxy>
ProxyPass /content balancer://balancer/
```

Starting with Apache 2.2, mod_proxy includes a new backend that enables load-balancing capabilities. The load balancing code is generic and allows you to balance multiple other protocols in addition to HTTP. To configure load balancing, first you need to define a group of backend servers with a <Proxy balancer://...> section, as shown here. Once defined, you can use the balancer ID with a regular ProxyPass directive. Each balancer ID and balancer member can take options to specify balancing strategies (based on traffic), fail over, connection pooling, and session support.

Finally, you can check the status of your load-balancing setup with the regular status handler and you can manipulate it with the balancer-manager handler.

Connecting to Tomcat

```
ProxyPass /myapp ajp://127.0.0.1:8009/myapp
ProxyPassReverse /myapp ajp://127.0.0.1:8009/myapp
```

Starting with Apache 2, mod_proxy includes an AJP protocol backend. The AJP protocol is commonly used by another Apache module, mod_jk, to communicate with application servers and servlet engines such as Tomcat and Jetty. It is now possible to replace mod_jk with the mod_proxy and mod_proxy_ajp modules, taking advantage of some of the newer functionality in mod_proxy such as load-balancing. As shown in the example, configuring AJP support in mod_proxy is as easy as replacing http:// with ajp:// in your proxy configurations (including load balancing setups).

Alternate Proxies

```
Squid http://www.squid-cache.org/
Pound http://www.apsis.ch/pound/
```

As explained in Chapter 9, "Performance and Scalability," Apache may not be the best choice for all scenarios. There are a number of other specialized proxy servers that may perform better than Apache, depending on your requirements. Two of the most popular open-source proxy servers are Pound and Squid. Squid has been around about as long as Apache, is highly configurable, and it excels in its caching abilities. Pound is a lightweight proxy server that is often used as an SSL reverse proxy.

Transparent HTTP Proxies

As mentioned earlier, a forward caching proxy requires that each client be properly configured. It is also possible to implement so-called transparent proxies. These machines intercept HTTP requests at the network layer and "transparently" serve them through a proxy server without the end-user noticing it. Transparent proxies are still popular with ISPs that want to cut down on bandwidth costs or control the surfing habits of their customers. Some organizations also use transparent proxies to filter spyware and viruses, as mentioned earlier in the "Enabling Forward Proxy Support" section. A typical transparent proxy setup involves using a transparent-proxying–aware server, such as Squid, and modifying your operating system's packet forwarding rules. You can learn more about setting up transparent HTTP proxies at the following Linux Documentation Project how to:

http://www.tldp.org/HOWTO/TransparentProxy.html

Multi Processing and Protocol Modules

The Evolution of Apache's Architecture

Apache is not a monolithic server. New modules can be added to provide enhanced functionality, and existing modules can be removed to reduce the size of the server and improve performance. Apache 2 takes this modularization concept further and introduces three new ways of extending the server:

- Multi Processing Modules (MPMs): Allow you to change the way Apache serves requests and improve the performance and scalability of the server.

- Filtering Modules: Provide a way for modules to process the content provided by other modules.

- Protocol Modules: The protocol layer has been abstracted, so it is possible for Apache to serve content using other protocols, such as FTP.

Selecting a Multi Processing Module

```
--with-mpm=worker
--with-mpm=prefork
```

Although MPM selection depends on many factors, including support for specific third-party modules and functionality, some MPMs perform better on certain platforms. For example, processes on AIX are "heavy" and a threaded MPM is preferred on this platform for scalability. It is not possible to change the request processing mechanism in Apache 1.3. For Apache 2, you select an MPM during the configuration and build process with the `--with-mpm` option. Currently, Windows has its own thread-based MPM, and Unix has two stable MPMs: prefork and worker. A number of additional modules are distributed with the server and considered experimental. The following sections explain the features of the different MPMs and how to configure them.

Understanding Process-Based MPMs

In a process-based server, the server forks several children. Forking means that a parent process makes identical copies of itself, called children. Each one of the children can serve a request independently of the others. This approach has the advantage of improved stability; if one of the children misbehaves, for example, by leaking memory, it can be killed without affecting the rest of the server.

The increased stability comes with a performance penalty: Each one of the children occupies additional memory, and the operating system spends a certain amount of time in context switching. In addition, this approach makes inter-process communication and data sharing difficult.

Apache 1.3 is a process-based server and Apache 2 provides a prefork MPM that allows it to perform as a process-based server. *Prefork* means that children can be forked at startup, instead of when a request comes. Apache allows you to configure the number of children to fork at startup and the maximum number of possible children, as described in the next section.

Configuring the Prefork MPM

```
StartServers 5
MinSpareServers 5
MaxSpareServers 10
MaxClients 150
MaxRequestsPerChild  0
```

You can control the number of processes that will be created at startup by using the StartServers directive. It takes a single argument, indicating the number of servers to fork when the server starts. The default value is 5 and is appropriate for most websites. You should change this setting only if you run a very busy website.

MaxClients enables you to control the maximum number of processes spawned, up to the operating system limits or Apache's maximum number of possible children. In Apache 1.3, the maximum number of possible children is hard coded to 256. To change this value, you will need to change the HARD_SERVER_LIMIT setting in httpd.h and recompile the server. In Apache 2, it can be changed in the configuration using the ServerLimit directive.

The MinSpareServers directive defines the minimum number of processes that can be idle (not serving any request) at any time. If the number of idle servers goes below the setting of MinSpareServers, Apache will spawn additional children. Conversely, MaxSpareServers sets the maximum number of idle processes allowed. If the number of idle servers grows beyond this setting, some of them will be killed. The default values, shown in the example, should be enough for most servers.

Finally, you can limit the number of requests that a specific process will serve using the MaxRequestsPerChild directive. It does not count multiple requests reusing the same connection. As explained earlier in the chapter, this is useful to prevent memory leaks from becoming an issue with processes that are running for a long time. The server will kill the process and replace it with a new one after the specified number of requests. You can set MaxRequestsPerChild to 0 if you do not want processes to be killed after a specific number of requests.

Understanding Threaded and Hybrid MPMs

Threads are similar to processes, but they can share memory and data with other threads. This has the advantage that there is no context switching (threads are part of the same process), and the disadvantage that poorly written code can take the whole server down with it. This can happen because a misbehaving thread is able to overwrite and corrupt data and code that belongs to other threads.

The Apache MPM for the Windows platform is an example of a threaded server MPM. Both threaded and process-based servers have their own sets of advantages and disadvantages. The Apache developers created a threaded MPM named *Worker MPM* that allows for a mixed approach. A server can spawn different processes, each one of them containing a number of threads.

Configuring the Worker MPM

```
StartServers 2
MaxClients 150
MinSpareThreads 25
MaxSpareThreads 75
ThreadsPerChild 25
MaxRequestsPerChild 0
```

The Worker MPM is an Apache 2 MPM that allows you to combine processes and threads. You can specify the number of processes that will be created at startup by using the StartServers directive, as with the Prefork MPM. Each of the processes will have several threads; how many each will have is specified by the ThreadsPerChild directive. The number of threads in each process is fixed, but processes are created or destroyed to maintain the total number of threads between specified limits. Those limits can be configured using MinSpareThreads and MaxSpareThreads. These directives are the counterparts of the MaxSpareServers and MinSpareServers directives in process-based servers.

Apache monitors the total number of threads across all processes and creates or destroys processes accordingly. As in Prefork, MaxClients specifies the maximum number of processes. In the Worker MPM, each process has several threads in turn, so the maximum number of simultaneous clients is MaxClients times the setting of ThreadsPerChild. MaxThreadsPerChild specifies the maximum number of threads per process and can be changed between restarts. ThreadLimit specifies an upper limit that cannot be changed between restarts. The StartServers and MaxClients directives are identical to the ones described in the section named "Configuring the Prefork MPM."

Using Alternate MPMs

```
--with-mpm=event
--with-mpm=perchild
```

Apache 2 includes a number of additional MPMs that are classified as experimental. Two of the most interesting ones are the Event MPM and the Perchild MPM. The Event MPM, present only in Apache 2.1, is a variant of the Worker MPM. In this MPM, a separate thread handles all listening sockets and keep-alive connections. This significantly increases scalability, as it allows the remaining threads to process requests instead of waiting for a client to close a connection or issue a new request. This MPM solves some of the issues described in Chapter 10, "Apache Proxy and Caching Support." The Perchild MPM allows Apache to run different virtual hosts under separate user IDs. This can help improve security and provides an alternative to running separate server instances.

In addition to those, the Metux MPM provides an alternative to the Perchild MPM. It can be downloaded from http://www.metux.de/mpm.

Understanding Apache 2 Filters

```
<Directory /usr/local/apache/htdocs/>
SetOutputFilter INCLUDES;PHP
</Directory>
AddOutputFilter INCLUDES .inc .shtml
```

You can think about the filtering architecture in Apache as a factory assembly line. Filters are workers in the factory, and requests and responses are the items traveling in the line. Each filter processes the content and passes the result to the next filter. Filters can process the information in a variety of ways, and a number of Apache modules are implemented as filters, such as SSL, Server Side Includes, and compression. Filters can be automatically added by modules at runtime or set up in the configuration file. This example shows how to use SetOutputFilter to add two filters to all documents under a particular directory and AddOutputFilter to associate filters with particular file extensions. Additionally, AddOutputFilterByType can be used to associate filters with specific file types.

If several directives, such as AddOutputFilter and SetOutputFilter, apply to the same file, the filter lists from both directives will be merged. Input filters can be configured via the AddInputFilter, AddInputFilterBytype, and SetInputFilter directives, which have identical syntax to their output filter counterparts.

Apache 2.1/2.2 includes mod_filter, which provides increased flexibility in defining and manipulating filter chains. This can be done, for example, based on the existence of a particular HTTP header or environment variable.

Using Apache As an FTP Server

```
Listen 10.0.0.1:21
<VirtualHost 10.0.0.1:21>
FTP On
DocumentRoot /usr/local/apache/ftpdocs
ErrorLog /usr/local/apache/logs/ftp_error_log
<Location />
    AuthName "FTP"
    AuthType basic
    AuthUserFile /usr/local/apache/conf/htusers
    Require valid-user
</Location>
</VirtualHost>
```

As mentioned earlier in this chapter, Apache 2 is more than a web server—it is a generic server framework. By building a server on top of Apache, a developer can take advantage of a solid, portable infrastructure; an extension mechanism; and the possibility of using many other third-party modules that exist for Apache. That is the case for mod_ftp, which adds FTP capabilities to Apache. Most of the configuration settings, such as authentication directives, are shared with the rest of the server. You can enable FTP support simply by adding FTP On inside the appropriate Virtual Host section. Additional directives, such as FTPUmask, FTPTimeoutLogin, FTPBannerMessage, and FTPMaxLoginAttempts, allow you to configure features common with other FTP servers.

At the time of this writing, mod_ftp is in the process of becoming an official ASF project and can be downloaded from http://incubator.apache.org/projects/mod_ftp.html.

Using Apache As a POP3 Server

```
Listen 110
<VirtualHost *:110>
POP3Protocol on
POP3MailDrops /usr/local/apache/pop
<Directory /usr/local/apache/pop>
  AuthUserFile /usr/local/apache/conf/htusers
  AuthName pop3
  AuthType Basic
  Require valid-user
</directory>
</VirtualHost>
```

This module allows Apache 2 to act as a POP3 server. POP3 stands for Post Office Protocol, version 3, and is a commonly used protocol that allows mail clients (such as Outlook, Eudora, or Netscape Mail) to retrieve messages from a central server. Note that this module will not allow your mail reader to send messages. For that you will need a SMTP (Simple Mail Transfer Protocol) server such as Sendmail or PostFix. You enable support for POP3 by placing a POP3Protocol On directive inside the appropriate virtual host container. POP3MailDrops specifies the location of the user's mailboxes. The user Apache is running as must be able to read and write to those mailboxes.

You can download mod_pop3 from http://svn.apache.org/viewcvs.cgi/httpd/mod_pop3/.

Compressing Content on the Fly

```
#Apache 2 mod_deflate
AddOutputFilterByType DEFLATE text/html text/plain
     text/xml
SetEnvIfNoCase Request_URI \.(?:gif|jpe?g|png)$
     no-gzip dont-vary
BrowserMatch ^Mozilla/4 gzip-only-text/html
#Apache 1.3 mod_gzip
mod_gzip_static_suffix .gz
AddEncoding gzip .gz
mod_gzip_item_include file \.html$
```

The mod_deflate filtering module included with Apache 2 provides a filter, DEFLATE, that can compress outgoing data. Compressing can be expensive in terms of CPU, but has the advantage of minimizing the amount of data that will be transferred to the client. This is useful when clients connect to the Internet via slow links and the content can be compressed significantly, such as with HTML pages. Other content that is already compressed, such as ZIP files or JPEG images, will benefit very little (if at all) from additional compression. Of course, for content compression to work, the client must support the opposite functionality: decompression. This is true for most modern browsers.

If you know that a specific client has trouble processing compressed content of a certain type, you can set up the environment variable no-gzip by using the SetEnvIf or BrowserMatch directive. This will prevent mod_deflate from compressing the content delivered to the client, as shown in the example.

Apache 1.3 has an equivalent module, mod_gzip, that can compress dynamic and static content: http://sourceforge.net/projects/mod-gzip/.

Index

How can we make this index more useful? Email us at indexes@samspublishing.com

M

How can we make this index more useful? Email us at indexes@samspublishing.com

How can we make this index more useful? Email us at indexes@samspublishing.com

215

Q–R

How can we make this index more useful? Email us at indexes@samspublishing.com

How can we make this index more useful? Email us at indexes@samspublishing.com

INDEX

219

T

How can we make this index more useful? Email us at indexes@samspublishing.com

221